100 WALKS IN
SOUTHWEST ENGLAND

Produced by AA Publishing
© AA Media Limited 2010

Published by AA Publishing (a trading name of AA Media Limited, whose registered office is Fanum House, Basing View, Basingstoke, Hampshire RG21 4EA; registered number 06112600)

This product includes mapping data licensed from Ordnance Survey® with the permission of the Controller of Her Majesty's Stationery Office.
© Crown copyright 2010. All rights reserved. Licence number 100021153

ISBN: 978-0-7495-6501-5
A04143

A CIP catalogue record for this book is available from the British Library.
The contents of this book are believed correct at the time of printing. Nevertheless, the publishers cannot be held responsible for any errors or omissions or for changes in the details given in this book or for the consequences of any reliance on the information it provides. We have tried to ensure accuracy, but things do change and we would be grateful if readers would advise us of any inaccuracies they encounter. This does not affect your statutory rights.

We have taken all reasonable steps to ensure that these walks are safe and achievable by walkers with a realistic level of fitness. However, all outdoor activities involve a degree of risk and the publishers accept no responsibility for any injuries caused to readers whilst following these walks. For more advice on using this book see page 11 and walking safely see page 112. The mileage range shown on the front cover is for guidance only – some walks may exceed or be less than these distances.

These routes appear in the AA Local Walks series and *1001 Walks in Britain*.

theAA.com/shop

Printed in China by Leo Paper Group

Picture credits
All images are held in the Automobile Association's own photo library (AA World Travel Library) and were taken by the following photographers:
Front cover J Wood; 3 J Tims; 6/7 M Jourdan; 9 A Burton; 10 G Edwardes.

Opposite: Ebbor Gorge, Somerset

Contents

Southwest England

The southwest is defined by its coastline, its villages and its country towns rather than by great cities or industrial conurbations. Even the metropolitan centres reflect the culture of rural and maritime England.

Southwest England

Surrounded by the South West Coast Path National Trail, the maritime influence is great here, but less than a third of the walks go anywhere near to the sea. The rest are in the downland and valleys of Dorset and Wiltshire, in pastoral farmland, picturesque villages, on the moors of Somerset and Devon or on the wetlands of the Levels.

The southwest has two national parks: wild Dartmoor and the cliffs and heaths of Exmoor. Protected Areas of Outstanding Natural Beauty encompass large stretches of the Cornish coast and Bodmin Moor, parts of Devon and Dorset, the Quantock Hills in Somerset and the North Wessex Downs in Wiltshire. There are also lengths of Heritage Coast with dramatic landscapes and a rich history. Further inland, the rural landscapes include Dorset, Wiltshire and Somerset.

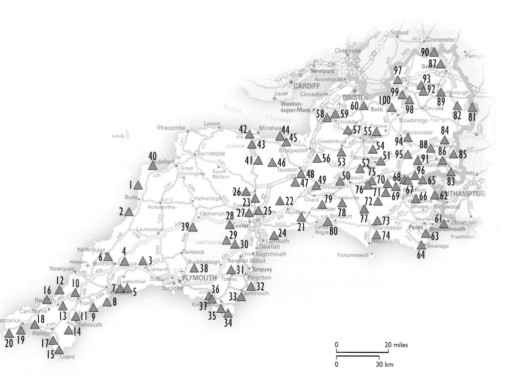

The Cornish Coast

Of the southwest coastline, the Cornish coast is probably the best-known section. In the north of the county, Morwenstow is associated with the Reverend R S Hawker, an eccentric vicar from Victoria's reign, while Crackington Haven draws students from all over the world to study the swirls and folds in its metamorphic rocks. Superlatives can be used to describe nearly every step of coastal path, and the walks explore not just idyllic rocky inlets, such as those at Prussia Cove, but also the subtropical backwaters of the Helford River and the defence systems that have guarded the Fal and Plymouth Sound for centuries. The coast, from Minehead in Somerset to Studland in Dorset, is circumnavigated by the South West Coast Path, Britain's longest National Trail, which we have incorporated into circular walks.

You'll need a head for heights if you are to make your way comfortably along the clifftops above St Agnes Head or the Dodman. As you thread your way along old coastguard paths you will wonder that anyone scratched a living out of these inhospitable climes. But the ancient fields bear witness to many centuries of occupation, and

when the industrial revolution brought new steam engines, the tin mines too were able to eke out an existence here.

The Devon Coast

Devon's coastal front is split in two. To the south, you'll find a continuation of the Cornish themes, though as the Dart, the Erme, the Avon, the Yealm and the Kingsbridge Estuary bite into the farmland of the South Hams, you're walking through an landscape of creeks and charming villages. The ferryfolk will become your friends if you are trying to join up the sections of the coastal path here. And at Bigbury-on-Sea you'll find they drive the most peculiar craft to get you to the offshore oasis of Burgh Island. There are no such problems awaiting you on the north Devon coast. If you negotiate the lanes to Clovelly in high season, you may rue its popularity, but venture from there on foot and you will soon leave the crowds behind.

Pages 6–7: Rock formation at Durdle Door, Dorset

Left: Off Hengistbury Head, Dorset

Somerset, Dorset and Wiltshire

In Somerset you'll discover wooded coombs linking the uplands with the sea below. At East Quantoxhead is the final piece of coastal scenery you will encounter in the northern part of the region. Dorset puts its own spin on the theme of up and down coastal paths. The highest up is on Golden Cap, sitting proudly above 627ft (191m) of fragile sandstone cliff. Like many walks here, though, you must get there from sea level – at Seatown in this case. In Purbeck, perhaps one of the loveliest parts of Dorset, a walk at Studland

will give you gentle sea-level rambling as far as Bournemouth and Hengistbury Head.

Inland, Wiltshire is littered with ancient remains, but nothing compares with the ritual landscape of Avebury, where the purpose of the earthworks and alignments of stones continue to remain a mystery.

Peculiar Shapes and Mysterious Lumps

The giant man at Cerne Abbas is certainly the rudest monument you'll encounter on these walks, and you will be able to make a study of pre-Roman fortifications. Badbury Rings and Cadbury Castle are perhaps the most extensive, the promontory forts of West Cornwall the most dramatic, and Burrow Mump, above the Somerset Levels, the most singular.

Moorland Wilderness

The remains of settlements on Dartmoor and Exmoor can be traced back over 4,000 years to the Bronze Age, and these lonely moorlands escaped the rigours of agricultural change. That's not to say recent human impact has not been great on the

moors of the southwest. Whether you're tracing the quarry tramways on Bodmin Moor, crossing the great dam at Meldon Reservoir, below Dartmoor's highest peaks, or listening to the eerie rattle of the nightjar in the plantations above Wimbleball Lake, you may reflect on the delicate balance between despoiling and enhancing our environment.

Battle Remains

The region has not been without conflict over the centuries. You'll find civil war stories at Nunney, Badbury, Wardour and Winyard's Gap. At Wells, and many other towns, you can learn of the Bloody Assizes, the cruel retribution meted out by James II's henchman Judge Jeffries, following the disastrous rising led by the Duke of Monmouth in 1685. The coast is littered with reminders of the Second World War – pill boxes like those overlooking the entrance to Plymouth Sound, which would have been manned by reservists had an invasion happened. The only invasion the southwest has to deal with now is the tourists who flood in every summer to surf and sun bathe. These walks will help you venture away into the real southwest of England.

Using this Book

➊ Information panels

Information panels show the total distance and total amount of ascent (that is the accumulated height you will ascend throughout the walk). An indication of the gradient you will encounter is shown by the rating 0–3. Zero indicates fairly flat ground and 3 indicates undulating terrain with several very steep slopes.

➋ Minimum time

The minimum time suggested is for approximate guidance only. It assumes reasonably fit walkers and doesn't allow for stops.

➌ Start points

The start of each walk is given as a six-figure grid reference prefixed by two letters indicating which 100km square of the National Grid it refers to. You'll find more information on grid references on most Ordnance Survey maps.

❹ Abbreviations

Walk directions use these abbreviations:

L – left
L–H – left-hand
R – right
R–H – right-hand
**Names which appear on signposts
are given in brackets, for example
('Bantam Beach').**

❺ Suggested maps

Details of appropriate maps are given for each walk, and usually refer to 1:25,000 scale Ordnance Survey Explorer maps. We strongly recommend that you always take the appropriate OS map with you. The maps in this book are there to give you the route and do not show all the details or relief that you will need to navigate around the routes provided in this collection. You can purchase Ordnance Survey Explorer maps at all good bookshops.

❻ Car parking

Many of the car parks suggested are public, but occasionally you may find you have to park on the roadside or in a lay-by. Please be considerate when you leave your car, ensuring that access roads or gates are not blocked and that other vehicles can pass safely. Remember that pub car parks are private and should not be used unless you are visiting the pub or you have the landlord's permission to park there.

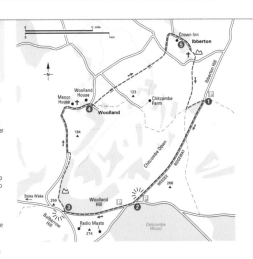

00

County • REGION

LOCATION Walk title
From the tops of Bulbarrow Hill to the valley floor and back, via an atmospheric church.

4.25 miles/6.8km 2hrs **Ascent** 591ft/180m ▲ **Difficulty** ①
Paths Quiet roads, muddy bridleways, field paths, 2 stiles
Map OS Explorer 117 Cerne Abbas & Bere Regis **Grid ref** ST 791071
Parking Car park at Ibberton Hill picnic site

❶ Turn **L** along road, following Wessex Ridgeway, with Ibberton laid out below to **R**. Road climbs gradually, and you see masts on Bulbarrow Hill ahead.
❷ After 1 mile (1.6km) pass car park on **L**, with plaque about Thomas Hardy. At junction bear **R** and immediately **R** again, signposted 'Stoke Wake'. Pass another car park on **R**. Woods of Woolland Hill now fall away steeply on **R**. Pass radio masts to **L** and reach small gate into field on **R**, near end of wood. Before taking it, go extra few steps to road junction ahead for wonderful view of escarpment stretching away west.
❸ Go through gate and follow uneven bridleway down. Glimpse spring-fed lake through trees on R. At bottom of field, path swings **L** to gate. Go through, on to road. Turn **R**, continuing downhill. Follow road into Woolland, passing Manor House and Old Schoolhouse, on **L** and **R** respectively.
❹ Beyond entrance, on **L**, to Woolland House turn **R** into lane and immediately **L** through kissing

gate. Path immediately forks. Take **L-H** track, down through marshy patches and young sycamores. Posts with yellow footpath waymarkers lead straight across meadow, with gorse-clad Chitcombe Down up **R**. Cross footbridge over stream. Go straight on to cross road. Keeping straight on, go through hedge gap. Bear **L** down field, cross stile and continue down. Cross footbridge and stile to continue along **L** side of next field. Go through gate to road junction. Walk straight up road ahead and follow it **R**, into Ibberton. Bear **R**.
❺ Continue up this road through village. This steepens and becomes path, bearing **R**. Steps lead up to church. Continue up steep path. Cross road and go straight ahead through gate. Keep straight on along fence, climbing steadily. Cross under power lines, continue in same direction, climbing steadily. Carry on open pasture to small gate in hedge. Do not go through gate, but turn sharp **L**, up slope, to small gate opposite car park.

112

Opposite: Scorhill Stone Circle, Chagford, Dartmoor National Park, Devon

MORWENSTOW The Parson-Poet

A walk in the footsteps of the eccentric Victorian poet, Robert Stephen Hawker.

7 miles/11.3km 4hrs **Ascent** 1,640ft/500m △ **Difficulty** 3
Paths Generally good, but inland paths and tracks can be very muddy during wet weather
Map OS Explorer 126 Clovelly & Hartland **Grid ref** SS 206154
Parking Small free car park by Morwenstow Church and Rectory Farm & Tea Rooms

❶ Follow signposted track from car park and church to coast path; turn **L**. Reach Hawker's Hut in about 100yds (91m). Continue along coast path to Duckpool.
❷ Reach inlet of Duckpool, walk up road along the bottom of valley to T-junction. Turn **L**. Turn **R** at next junction to cross bridge beside ford. Follow lane round **L** for 150yds (137m), then bear **L** on broad track through woodland.
❸ After 1 mile (1.6km), cross stile on **L**, cross wooden footbridge, climb slope, then turn **R** and up track. Turn **L** at T-junction, keep ahead at next junction. In 40yds (37m) go **R** through metal gate.
❹ Follow signed field track to lane at Woodford. Turn **L**, go downhill past Shears Farm then round **R** and uphill to junction with road. Turn **L** past bus shelter.
❺ After 100yds (91m), turn **L** along path between cottages to kissing gate. Turn **R**, immediately **L** and follow edge of field to stile on **L**. Cross stile, then cross next field to hedge opposite.

❻ Cross 2 stiles; go straight up next field (often muddy) to hedge corner. Go alongside wall and over stile to hedged track and on to junction with lane.
❼ Go through gate opposite; turn **R** through gap. Bear **L** across field to stile. Keep straight across next field to top left-hand corner; go through gate up to Stanbury House. Turn **R** to reach surfaced lane.
❽ Go **L** along lane (few paces) then over narrow stile on **R**. Go straight across next 2 fields to kissing gate into farm lane behind Tonacombe House.
❾ Keep ahead through kissing gate, then along muddy track and through another. Cross 2 fields; descend into wooded valley. Keep **R,** cross stream, go **R** and up steeply to kissing gate.
❿ Cross fields to garden behind Bush Inn. Go down the **L-H** side of buildings, then up to road. Turn **L** for Morwenstow Church and car park.

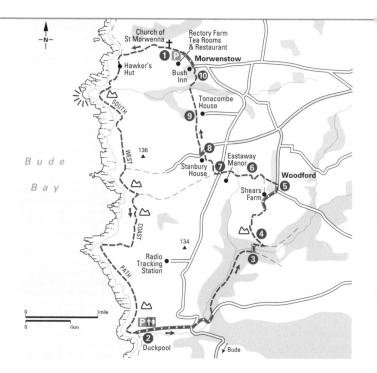

CRACKINGTON HAVEN A Geological Phenomenon

A coastal and inland walk with views of the spectacular sea cliffs of the North Cornish coast.

3.5 miles/5.7km 1hr 45min **Ascent** 270ft/82m ⚠ **Difficulty** ☐2

Paths Good coastal footpath and woodland tracks. Can be very wet and muddy

Map OS Explorer 111 Bude, Boscastle & Tintagel **Grid ref** SX 145969

Parking Crackington Haven car park. From the A39 at Wainhouse Corner, or from Boscastle on the B3263. Can be busy in summer. Burden Trust car park and picnic area

❶ From Crackington Haven car park entrance go **L** across bridge, then turn **R** at telephone kiosk. Follow broad track round to **L**, between signpost and old wooden seat, then go through kissing gate on to coast path.

❷ Eventually, stile leads to steep stepped descent to footbridges below Cambeak and path junction. Keep **L** and follow path up sheltered valley on inland side of steep hill, then continue on cliff path.

❸ At start of stretch of low inland cliff, pass coast path post marked 'Trevigue'. Turn **L** at next path to reach road by National Trust sign for 'Strangles'.

❹ Go **L**, past farm entrance to Trevigue, then, in few paces, turn **R** down drive by Trevigue sign. Then bear off to **L** across grass to go through gate with yellow arrow.

❺ Go directly down field, keeping **L** of telegraph pole, to reach stile. Continue downhill to stile on edge of wood. Continue down tree-shaded path to junction of paths in shady dell by river.

❻ Turn sharp **L** here, following signpost towards Haven, and continue on obvious path down to wooded river valley.

❼ Cross footbridge, then turn **L** at junction with track. Cross another footbridge, continue to gate by some houses. Follow track and then surfaced lane to main road, then turn **L** to car park.

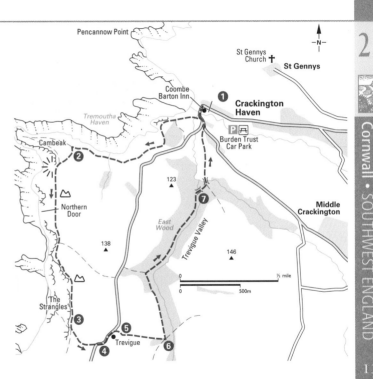

BODMIN MOOR Rocky Bounds

A walk across the wilds of Bodmin Moor.

3 miles/4.8km 2hrs **Ascent** 230ft /70m ⚠ **Difficulty** 1
Paths Moorland tracks and paths and disused quarry tramways
Map OS Explorer 109 Bodmin Moor **Grid ref** SX 260711
Parking The Hurlers car park on southwest side of Minions village

❶ Leave car park by steps at top end beside information board about The Hurlers stone circles. Cross grass to broad stony track. Turn **R** and follow track, passing The Hurlers circles on **R** and Pipers stones further on.

❷ At 3-way junction, by large granite block, take **R-H** track down through shallow valley bottom, then climb uphill on green track towards Cheesewring Quarry. At junction with another track, cross over and follow grassy track uphill towards quarry. At 1st green hillock, go sharp **R**, then round **L** to Daniel Gumb's Cave. Return to path and follow it uphill alongside fenced-in rim of quarry to Cheesewring rock formation.

❸ Retrace steps towards shallow valley bottom.

❹ Short distance from valley bottom, abreast of thorn trees on **R** and just before fenced-off mound on **L**, turn off **R** along path. Keep **L** of thorn trees and big leaning block of granite and soon pick up faint beginnings of grassy track. Follow track, keeping to **R** of thorn tree and gorse bushes. Track becomes clearer.

❺ Track begins to strand. At leaning rock, split like whale's mouth, keep **R** along path through scrub and with rocky heights of Sharp Tor in line ahead. Keep to path round slope, with Wardbrook Farm **L** and Sharp Tor ahead. Reach surfaced road and turn **R** for few paces to open gateway.

❻ Go to **R** of fence by gateway and follow path alongside fence past 2 slim granite pillars. Join disused tramway and follow this.

❼ Pass some big piles of broken rock and, about 30yds (27m) beyond, turn sharp **R** at wall corner. Follow green track uphill and alongside wall. Where wall ends keep on uphill to reach broad track.

❽ Turn **R** along track to visit Cheesewring Quarry. For main route, turn **L** and follow track to Minions village. Pass Minions Heritage Centre, converted mine engine house. At main road, turn **R** through village to return to car park.

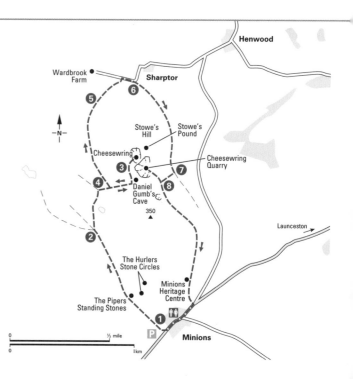

CARDINHAM Through The Woods

A long woodland walk in quiet countryside.

5 miles/8km 3hrs **Ascent** 328ft/100m ⚠ **Difficulty** 1
Paths Generally clear woodland tracks and field sections, 6 stiles
Map OS Explorer 109 Bodmin Moor **Grid ref** SX 099666
Parking Cardinham Woods car park

❶ Cross wooden bridge over Cardinham Water, pass café and play area. Bear **R**, then **R** again through barrier to 3-way junction. Keep **R**, follow forestry track through woods. (Cardinham Water **R**.)

❷ At junction of tracks, bear **R**, cross stream descending from **L**, then turn **L** up unmarked track. Pass picnic tables by rock face on bend.

❸ Just before bridge turn **R** at junction just before marker post. In few paces, at next junction, keep ahead along track through Lidcutt Wood. Cross stile, continue through woods.

❹ Emerge into field; right of way heads across field for wooden gate on to concrete track. Turn **L** and follow track to public road. Turn **R**, follow road over brow of the hill and down into valley.

❺ Pass lane junction and keep ahead downhill to cross river; go **R** at public footpath sign. Cross ditch and stile. Head diagonally up field, aiming to **R** of Cardinham church tower, to stile. Go along grassy ride beside church. Turn **R** at road.

❻ At public footpath sign opposite cemetery, go **R** and through gate into field. Keep ahead for 50yds (46m), then bear **L** across field by white house. Follow rough grassy track, keeping **L** of tree. Go through 2 metal gates and keep alongside hedge on **R**. Where track bends round **R**, bear **L** at footpath post, head downhill between trees and cross meadow to stile. This is line of right of way.

❼ Bear slightly **L** across next field to wooden gate beside horse jump. Keep ahead through meadow to bridge over stream by water jump, then follow path through trees. Go through wooden gate and reach T-junction with lane at Milltown. Turn **R**, down lane, and keep **L** at junction. Pass Milltown Farm, then pass junction on **L** and reach wooden barrier. Go up slope, then turn **R** at junction with forestry track.

❽ Follow track, pass Lady Vale Bridge and join lane from Target Cottage, to return to car park.

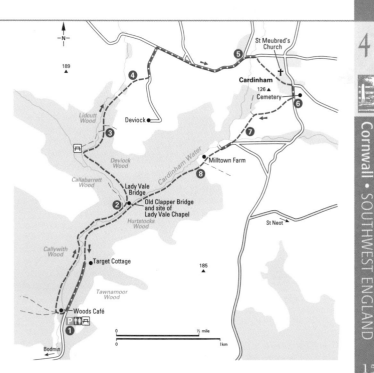

POLRUAN A Glimpse Of Old Cornwall

A woodland and coastal walk from the village of Polruan through the ancient parish of Lanteglos.

4 miles/6.4km 3hrs 30min **Ascent** 754ft/230m ⚠ **Difficulty** 2

Paths Good throughout. Can be very muddy in woodland areas during wet weather

Map OS Explorer 107 St Austell & Liskeard **Grid ref** SX 126511

Parking Polruan. An alternative start to the walk can be made from the National Trust Pencarrow car park (Point ④ SX 149513). Also at Fowey's Central car park, then catch the ferry to Polruan

① Walk up from Quay at Polruan, then turn **L** along East Street, by telephone box and seat. Go **R**, up steps, signposted 'To the Hills' and 'Hall Walk'. Go **L** at next junction, then keep along path ahead. Keep **R** at junction and pass National Trust sign, 'North Downs'. ② Turn **R** at T-junction with track. In few paces, bear off **L** along path, signposted 'Pont and Bodinnick'. Reach wooden gate on to lane. Don't go through gate, but instead bear **L** and go through footgate. Follow path, established by National Trust, and eventually descend steep wooden steps. ③ At T-junction with track, turn **R** and climb uphill. (It's worth diverting **L** at the T-junction to visit Pont.) On this route, reach lane. Go **L** for few paces then, on bend by Little Churchtown Farm, bear off **R** through gate signed 'Footpath to Church'. Climb steadily to reach Church of St Winwaloe. ④ Turn **L** outside church and follow narrow lane. At T-junction, just beyond Pencarrow car park, cross

road and go through gate, then turn **R** along field edge on path established by National Trust, to go through another gate. Turn **L** along field edge. ⑤ At field corner, turn **R** on to coast path and descend very steeply. (To continue to Pencarrow Head go **L** over stile and follow path on to headland. From here coast path can be rejoined and access made to Great Lantic Beach.) Follow coast path for about 1.25 miles (2km), keeping to cliff edge ignoring any junctions. ⑥ Where cliff path ends, go through gate to road junction. Cross road then go down School Lane. Turn **R** at 'Speakers Corner', then turn **L** down Fore Street to reach Quay at Polruan.

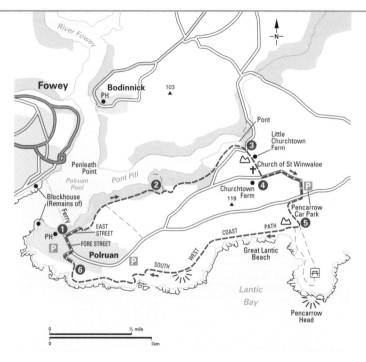

WADEBRIDGE Along The Banks Of The River Camel

A gentle walk along the famous old railway trackbed of the Camel Trail and through woodlands.

6 miles/9.7km 3hrs 30min **Ascent** 328ft/100m ⚠ **Difficulty** 1

Paths Farm and forestry tracks and well-surfaced old railway track
Map OS Explorer 106 Newquay and Padstow **Grid ref** SW 991722
Parking Wadebridge main car park near the bridge. Small parking area at end of Guineaport Road at start of the Camel Trail

❶ From car parks in Wadebridge, walk along Southern Way Road past Betjeman Centre and continue along Guineaport Road following Camel Trail. Start from end of road if using adjacent parking.
❷ Do not follow Camel Trail. Instead, keep **R** at fork and within few paces, at junction, where road curves up to **R**, keep ahead along unsurfaced track signposted 'Public Footpath to Treraven'. Follow track steadily uphill. Go through wooden gate and follow **R-H** field edge to go through another gate. Continue along track to reach junction in front of Treraven farm.
❸ Go **L** and follow track as it bears R; then, in about 15yds (14m), at junction, keep **R** and then **L** and continue along track to reach bend on minor public road by house.
❹ Keep straight ahead along road, with care, then turn **L** at cross roads, signposted 'Burlawn'. At next junction, bear **L** and follow road through Burlawn. Go steeply downhill on narrow tree-lined lane.

❺ At Hustyn Mill, beyond little footbridge, turn **L** off road and follow broad woodland track through Bishops Wood. Stay on main track to where it reaches surfaced road at Polbrock Bridge.
❻ Turn **L** over bridge across River Camel and, in few paces, go off **L** and down steps to join Camel Trail. Turn **L** here and follow unwavering line of Camel Trail back to Wadebridge.

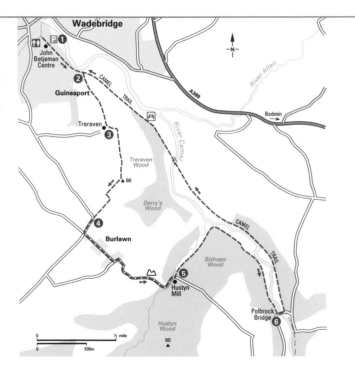

FOWEY Daphne du Maurier's World
In the footsteps of Daphne du Maurier.

7.5 miles/12km 4hrs **Ascent** 820ft/250m ⚠ **Difficulty** 2
Paths Field paths, rough lanes and coastal footpath, can be very muddy on inland tracks during wet weather; 10 stiles **Map** OS Explorer 107 St Austell & Liskeard **Grid ref** SX 118511 **Parking** Readymoney Cove car park, reached by continuing on from entrance to Fowey's main car park

❶ From bottom end of car park walk down St Catherine's Parade; turn **R** towards Readymoney Cove. Continue to end of road, above beach; follow rocky Love Lane up on Saints Way. Go past 1st junction, ignoring options by NT sign for 'Covington Woods'.
❷ Turn **L** at next junction and then climb wooden steps to reach Allday's Fields. Follow **R-H** field edge. At field gap follow obvious grassy track ahead to lane end at Coombe Farm. Follow lane ahead.
❸ At road, turn **R** and continue to Lankelly Farm. Pass junction on **R** and follow Prickly Post Lane for few paces. Turn off **L** on to gravel drive, then keep **L** and along narrow fenced-in path.
❹ After barn conversions at Trenant, cross lane, then stile. Keep ahead alongside field edge; follow path to kissing gate into field below Tregaminion Farm. Go up field to gate, continue between buildings then turn **R**, then **L**, to reach T-junction with road by entrance gate to little Church of Tregaminion.

❺ Turn **R** and in 100yds (91m) go **L** into field. Reach junction on edge of some woods. (For enjoyable diversion, take **R-H** branch to beach and cove at Polkerris.) On main route, keep **L** along field edge and follow well-defined coast path for 1.25 miles (2km) to Gribbin Head.
❻ Enter wooded National Trust property of Gribbin. Keep **L** at junction. Go through gate and cross to Gribbin Daymark. Go **L** and down faint grassy track, then follow coast path along to Polridmouth.
❼ Follow coast path and at open ground, follow seaward field edge. Go steeply in to, and out of, Coombe Hawne. Enter Covington Wood, keep **L** at immediate junction, and pass the Rashleigh Mausoleum.
❽ Turn **R** at junction to reach St Catherine's Castle. Return along path then go down steps at 1st junction on **R**. Go down wooden steps to reach Readymoney Beach. Return to car park via St Catherine's Parade.

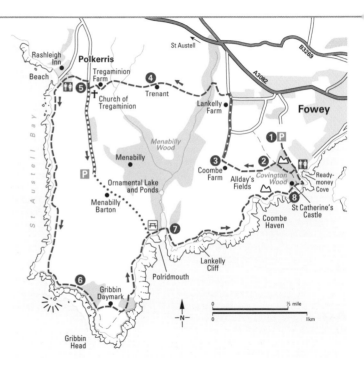

DODMAN POINT Ancient Walls

A circuit of the headland of Dodman Point.

4.5 miles/7.2km 3hrs **Ascent** 377ft/115m ⚠ **Difficulty** ☐1
Paths Good coastal paths. Inland paths can be muddy, 2 stiles
Map OS Explorer 105 Falmouth & Mevagissey **Grid ref** SX 011415
Parking Gorran Haven car park, pay at kiosk

❶ Turn **L** on leaving car park and walk down to Gorran Haven harbour. Just before access on to beach, turn **R** to walk up Fox Hole Lane, then go up steps, signposted 'Hemmick via Dodman'. Walk up more steps. Follow coast path ahead, past sign for National Trust property of Lamledra.
❷ Keep **L** at junction situated below rocky outcrop. (Steep alternative path leads up **R** from here, past memorial plaque, to rejoin main coast path.) On main route go down stone steps and follow path along slope. At junction, keep **R**. **L-H** track leads down to Vault Beach. Here regain coastal path by track leading uphill. Keep **L** at next junction.
❸ Go **L** through kissing gate and follow path through scrubland. Keep ahead at junction signed 'Dodman Point' then go through kissing gate on to open ground. Continue on footpath to summit of Dodman Point.
❹ Approaching the large granite cross on summit of Dodman, reach junction from where path going

R leads to The Watch House. Continue to cross on summit and then, just before cross and at next junction and arrow post, go **R** along coast path.
❺ Cross stile beyond gate with access notice pinned to it. Reach junction in few paces. Turn **R** and then follow path between high banks of Bulwark.
❻ Keep ahead where path comes in from **R**. Follow hedged track to reach kissing gate and surfaced lane at Penare. Turn **R** along lane.
❼ At junction leave road and go through field gate signposted 'Treveague'. Keep across 3 fields, then at road end by houses, turn **R**, signposted 'Gorran Haven'. Go **L** at signpost and go along drive behind house, bearing round **R**. Go **L** through gate and then along path above small valley.
❽ Cross muddy area by some stepping stones, then go through gate. Follow driveway ahead to T-junction with public road. Turn **R** and walk down, with care as there can be traffic, to Gorran Haven car park.

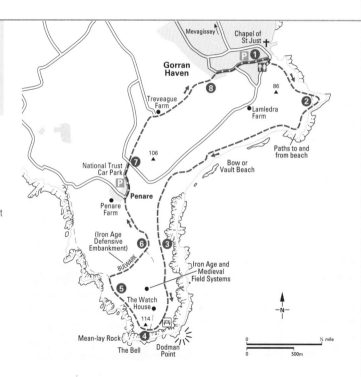

NARE HEAD Hidden Cornwall
Through fields and along the coast.

7 miles/11.3km 5hrs **Ascent** 1,312ft/400m ⚠ **Difficulty** 2

Paths Good coastal footpath, field paths and quiet lanes. Field stiles are often overgrown, 30 stiles

Map OS Explorer 105 Falmouth & Mevagissey **Grid ref** SW 906384

Parking Carne Beach car park. Large National Trust car park behind beach

❶ Turn **L** out of car park and walk up road, with care. Past steep bend, turn **R**, go up steps and on to coast path. Continue to Paradoe Cove and past Nare Head.

❷ Above Kiberick Cove go through gap in wall. Keep ahead through dip to reach stile. Follow coast path to Portloe. Go **L** up road from cove, past Ship Inn.

❸ Just after sharp **L-H** bend, where road narrows, cross high stile, **R**. Cross field to stile, then follow next field edge. Pass gate, then, in few paces, go **R** and over stile. Cross next field to stile into lane.

❹ Go **R** along road past Camels Farm for 200yds (183m), then go **L** over stile and follow field edge to stile. Follow next field edge, then just before field corner, go **R** over stile. Turn **L** through gap, then go diagonally **R** across next 2 fields to stile. At road junction, continue along road signposted 'Carne and Pendower'.

❺ Just past Tregamenna Manor Farm, on bend, go over stile by gate. Cut across corner of field, then go **R** over stile. Cross next field to stile and then continue to T-junction with lane. (Turn **R** to visit Veryan.)

❻ If not visiting village, turn **L**, then, just past Churchtown Farm, go **L** over stile. Follow filed-edge to stile into lane. Go immediately **L** over 2 stiles, then follow path, past Carne Beacon, to lane.

❼ At corner junction keep ahead down lane, signposted 'Carne Village Only'. Bear **R** down driveway past Beacon Cottage. Go through gate signposted 'Defined Footpaths Nos 44 & 45'. Follow track round to **R** between garage and house, then follow grassy track, keeping ahead at junction signposted 'Carne Beach'. Go through gate (dogs on leads here) and follow path alongside grassy bank and fence.

❽ Abreast of old wooden gate up on **R**, bear **L** and downhill through scrub, (path isn't evident at first), and soon pick up path through gorse to join coast path back to start.

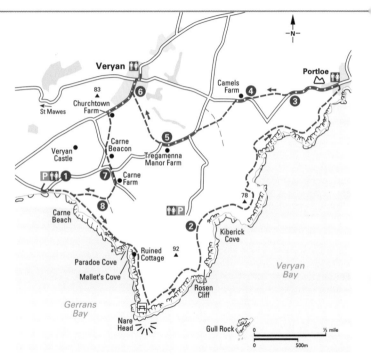

BISHOP'S WOOD A Forestry Estate

Enjoy the local flora and fauna on this short and gentle stroll through richly diverse woodlands near Truro.

3.5 miles/5.7km 2hrs 30min **Ascent** 164ft/50m ⚠ **Difficulty** 1
Paths Forest tracks and paths. Can be very muddy after rain. **Map** OS Explorer 105 Falmouth & Mevagissey **Grid ref** SW 820477 **Parking** Forestry car park, north of Idless, near Truro **NOTE:** Car park gates are closed at sunset. Working woodland, please take note of notices advising work in progress

❶ Leave top end of car park via wooden barrier and go along broad track. In few paces at fork, keep to **R** fork and follow track above Woodpark and along inside edge of wood. This track can be very muddy after rain.

❷ Keep ahead on main track, walking parallel to river, ignoring branch tracks leading off to **L**.

❸ Just before northern end of wood reach fork. Keep to main track as it bends **L** and uphill. Track levels off and at open area merges with broad forestry ride. Keep ahead along ride.

❹ At forestry notice indicating site of remains of Iron Age encampment, go **L** along path beneath conifer trees to reach bank and ditch of encampment. Return to the main track and turn **L**.

❺ At bend beside wooden bench, where tracks lead off to **L** and **R**, go **R** and follow public footpath uphill. At path crossing turn **L** and follow path through scrubland and young pine trees.

❻ Re-enter mature woodland and follow track downhill. Keep **R** at junction, then go **L** at next junction. Reach a T-junction with broad track. Turn **R** and follow track back to car park.

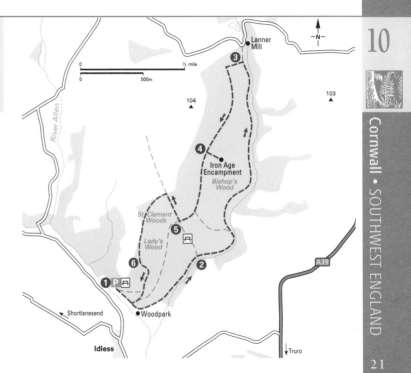

11

MYLOR CHURCHTOWN A Waterside Walk

To Flushing on a quiet peninsula dominated by ships and sails.

4 miles/6.4km 3hrs **Ascent** 164ft/50m ⚠ **Difficulty** 1
Paths Good paths throughout. Wooded section to Trelew Farm is often very wet, 7 stiles
Map OS Explorer 105 Falmouth & Mevagissey **Grid ref** SW 820352
Parking Mylor Churchtown car park

1 From car park entrance, turn **R** to reach surfaced lane, signed 'Flushing'. Follow lane; by gateway of house, bear **L** along path. Pass in front of Restronguet Sailing Club and keep to **R** of detached building.
2 Follow path round Penarrow Point and continue round Trefusis Point. Reach gate and granite grid stile by wooden shack at Kilnquay Wood. Continue to lane.
3 Follow lane round **L**, then go **R** through gap beside gate; continue along public road. Where road drops down to water's edge, bear **R** up surfaced slope to area of 'Bowling Green'. (Strictly no dog fouling.) Continue past little pavilion and toilets and go down surfaced path, then turn **L** at junction just after 2 seats.
4 Turn **R** at junction and go past Seven Stars Inn. At junction by Royal Standard Inn, keep **R** and go up Kersey Road. At top of road, by Orchard Vale, go **L** up steps, signed 'Mylor Church'. Cross stile; keep to field edge to isolated house and to stile of granite bollards.
5 In 25yds (23m) go **R** through gate, turn **L** over cattle grid and follow drive to public road, Penarrow

Road. Cross with care, and go down road opposite for 30yds (27m), then go **R** down steps and on down field edge.
6 Enter woodland and keep **R** at junction to follow rocky path often mini stream after heavy rainfall. Go through gate, keep ahead at junction then cross small stream. Go through tiny gate then turn **R** down farm track to surfaced lane at Trelew.
7 Turn **R** along lane, passing old water pump. At slipway, keep ahead along unsurfaced track. Continue along between granite posts and on to join public road into Mylor Churchtown. Cross road with care (blind corner) and go through churchyard of St Mylor Church (path through the churchyard is not public right of way). Turn **R** at waterfront to car park in Mylor Churchtown.

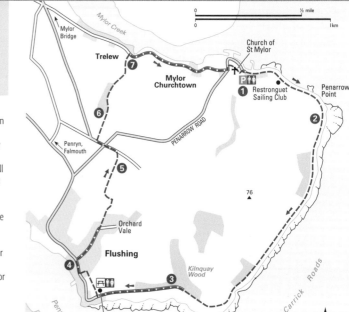

ST AGNES High Cliffs And A High Hill

A bracing walk along the cliffs at St Agnes, then inland to the top of St Agnes Beacon.

5 miles/8km 3hrs **Ascent** 623ft/190m ⚠ **Difficulty** ②
Paths Good coastal footpaths and inland tracks **Map** OS Explorer 104 Redruth & St Agnes
Grid ref SW 699514 **Parking** St Agnes Head.
Number of parking spaces along the clifftop track. Start the walk from any of these.

❶ Join coastal footpath from clifftop parking place. Follow stony track across Tubby's Head. Branch off **R** on to narrower path (acorn signpost) about 100yds (91m) before old mine buildings (remains of Wheal Coates mine). Cross stone stile and continue to Towanroath mine engine house.

❷ About 80yds (71m) beyond Towanroath branch off **R** at junction and continue to Chapel Porth Beach.

❸ Cross stream at back corner of car park and follow path up Chapel Combe. Keep straight ahead when main path bends sharp **R**. Pass below mine building and where path forks among trees, go **L** through wooden kissing gate.

❹ Turn **R** along track and where it bends **L** go **R** along another track. Pass some houses and where track narrows to path, keep ahead at fork. Go through gate and pass bench. Go along edge of field and eventually turn **L** through kissing gate on to wide track.

❺ At junction, turn **L** and then **R** at Willow Cottage and go up to public road. Turn **R** and keep ahead at next junction. In 200yds (183m), next to entrance of Beacon Country House Hotel, go up stony track on **L**. After 50yds (46m), at junction, turn **L**. Track becomes path just past cottage. At staggered junction keep straight uphill between telegraph poles to summit of St Agnes Beacon.

❻ From summit of Beacon follow the **L-H** track of 2 tracks, heading northwest down to road. Turn **R** along road to reach seat.

❼ Go down track opposite seat. Where track bends **R**, keep straight on down path directly to edge of cliffs, then turn **L** at junction with coast path and return to car park.

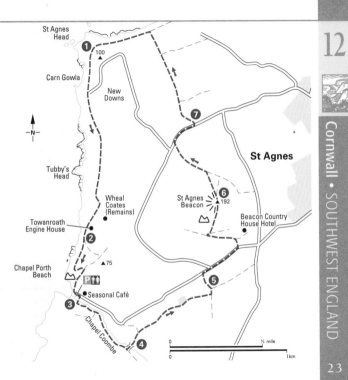

REDRUTH Mines And Methodism
Through Cornwall's mining heartland.

4 miles/6.4km 2hrs 30min **Ascent** 442ft/135m ⚠ **Difficulty** 1
Paths Field paths, rough tracks and surfaced lanes. Can be muddy after rain, 6 stiles
Map OS Explorer 104 Redruth & St Agnes **Grid ref** SW 699421
Parking Car parks in Redruth

❶ From any car park, walk to Fore Street, main street of Redruth. Continue to junction (railway station, **R**) and take middle branch, to **L** of Wesley Centenary Memorial Building (now YMCA) and signposted 'To Victoria Park'. This is Wesley Street. In few paces turn **R** on Sea View Terrace; chimney stack of Pednandrea Mine is **L**, just along road. Pass Basset Street on **R** and, where streets cross, go **L**, up Raymond Road to T-junction with Sandy Lane.

❷ Cross road with care; follow track opposite, signposted 'Public Bridleway' and 'Grambler Farm'. Go through gate by farm and continue to open area. Bear **L**, follow track between hedges. At junction with track turn **L**, signposted 'Gwennap Pit'.

❸ Go **R** and over stile next to field gateway with breeze block gateposts. Cross stile at next gate; keep ahead across field. Cross stile; continue between wire fences by house to stile. Go down lane to junction and follow road opposite for 100yds (91m) to Gwennap Pit.

❹ Follow road away from Gwennap Pit. Ignore 1st

few turn offs and in 300yds (274m) turn off to **R** along track, signposted 'Public Bridleway'. Keep ahead at 2 crossings, then, at final crossing beside ruined building, turn **R** and follow track up hill to summit of Carn Marth.

❺ Pass flooded quarry on **L**. Follow rocky path round to **R** past trig point and on along fenced-in rim of deep quarry. Keep ahead at junction and go down track to reach surfaced road. Turn **L** and in 30yds (27m) turn **L** along track, signed 'Public Bridleway'. Follow track to T-junction with main road at house (Tara). Cross with care, turn **R** and continue for 300yds (180m).

❻ Go **L** at junction, signposted as cycle route, and follow lane **R**, then **L** into avenue of houses. At crossroads turn **R** along Trefusis Road. At next junction turn **L** into Raymond Road and then turn **R** at next crossroads into Sea View Terrace. Turn **L** down Wesley Street and on into Fore Street.

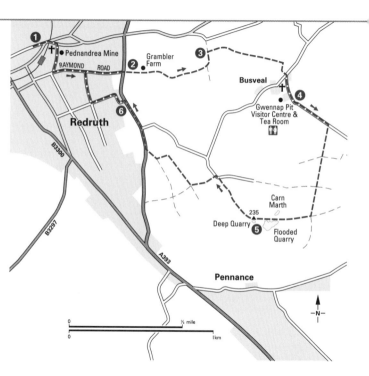

HELFORD Hidden Creeks

A circuit of peaceful tidal creeks.

5 miles/8km 3hrs **Ascent** 328ft/100m ⚠ **Difficulty** 1 **Paths** Good woodland paths and tracks and field paths. Short section of quiet lane, 10 stiles **Map** OS Explorer 103 The Lizard **Grid ref** SW 759261 **Parking** Helford car park. Large car park overlooking creek. Can become busy in summer. Only authorised cars are allowed beyond the car park into the village of Helford

❶ Turn **L** along path, signed 'Coast Path'. Go through metal gate and follow sunken track. Descend steps, then turn **R** along lane. At a steep R-H bend, bear off ahead along track. Follow this permissive path through trees, passing some fine little beaches.

❷ Leave wooded area via metal gate, then turn **L** along field edge to stone stile. Follow bottom edge of next 2 fields. Go through field gap beside white pole and post and triangle (navigation marks). Follow field edge ahead. Go through kissing gate, then follow field edge (seat and viewpoint on **L**). Go through kissing gate. Go **L** to start of wide grassy track between gorse and low trees. (For short circuit of Dennis Head, follow track to stile on **L**.)

❸ To continue on main route, turn sharply **R** at start of wide track and follow **L-H** field edge and then path across open field. Join track behind house, then go through kissing gate and descend to St Anthony's Church. Follow road alongside Gillan Creek. Part way along is National Trust path along creek edge.

❹ Just past where road curves round bay, go up **R** and through gate by public footpath sign. Follow broad track through trees to houses at Roscadden. Keep ahead along track to Manaccan at T-junction opposite Manaccan Church.

❺ Cross churchyard and then enter gate to road. Keep ahead to junction, New Inn is **L**, then go up **R**, past school. Keep uphill, then turn **L** along Minster Meadow, go over stile, and through field to road.

❻ Go diagonally **L** to stile opposite, cross field, then go **L** following signposts to reach woods. Follow path ahead. Reach junction with track going up **L**. Go over stile ahead. Reach another junction.

❼ Bear down **R** and follow broad track through trees to some buildings at Helford. Keep ahead at surfaced road and follow road uphill to car park.

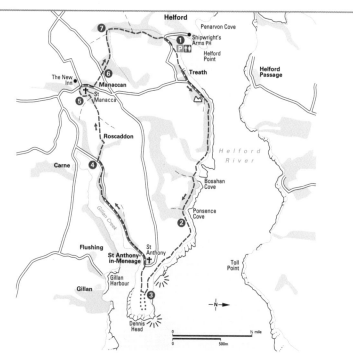

CADGWITH The Serpentine Route

A wandering route between coast and countryside through the landscape of the Lizard Peninsula.

4.5 miles/7.2km 3hrs **Ascent** 230ft/70m ⚠ **Difficulty** 1

Paths Very good. Occasionally rocky in places. Rock can be slippery when wet.

Map OS Explorer 103 The Lizard **Grid ref** SW 720146

Parking Cadgwith car park. About 350yds (320m) from Cadgwith. Busy in summer

❶ Go **L** along grassy ride below car park, to stile. Continue through gate and into woodland. Turn **R** at lane, then on corner, go up track and continue to main road at Ruan Minor.

❷ Go **L** and, just beyond shop, turn **L** down surfaced path. Rejoin main road by thatched cottage (there are toilets just before road). Cross diagonally **R**, then go down lane past Church of St Ruan.

❸ In 0.3 mile (500m), just past old mill and bridge, go **R** at T-junction to reach car park at Poltesco. From far end of car park follow track, signposted 'Carleon Cove'. Go **R** at junction.

❹ Go over wooden bridge above cove, then turn **L** at T-junction and again turn **L** in 0.25 mile (400m) where path branches. Go through kissing gate and continue along cliff-edge path to Cadgwith. At road, turn **L**.

❺ Follow narrow path, signposted 'Coast Path'. By house gateway, go **L** up surfaced path, signposted 'Devil's Frying Pan'. At open area turn **L**, pass

Townplace Cottage, cross meadow and reach Devil's Frying Pan itself.

❻ Keep on coast path and at junction, just past chalet studio, follow path inland to T-junction with rough track. Turn **L** and then, at public lane, go **L** again and after 0.5 mile (800m) turn **R** along track to Grade Church.

❼ Follow **L-H** field edge behind church, then go over stile into next field to reach lane. St Ruan's Well is opposite diagonally **L**. Turn **R** for 200yds (183m), then branch off **R** between stone pillars to return to car park.

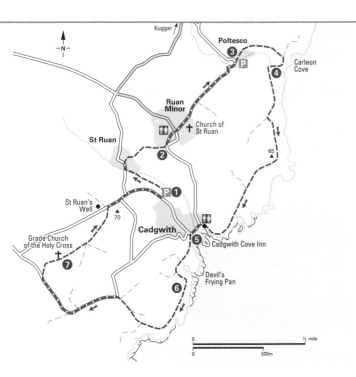

PORTREATH Cliffs And Deep Woods

Along spectacular cliffs and through shady woods.

4 miles/6.4km 3hrs **Ascent** 459ft/140m ⚠ **Difficulty** ②

Paths Good coastal path, woodland path, farm tracks
Map OS Explorer 104 Redruth & St Agnes **Grid ref** SW 654453
Parking Portreath Beach, Basset's Cove, North Cliffs, Tehidy Country Park, East Lodge

❶ Cross bridge opposite Portreath Beach car park; turn **R** up Battery Hill, signposted 'Coast Path'. Follow lane uphill and to end at houses above beach. Go **L** in front of garages, signposted 'Coast Path Gwithian'.
❷ Follow path through gate and then keep straight uphill to cliff top. Don't go close to cliff edge. Turn **L** and follow path round cliff edge above Ralph's Cupboard. Continue by steep paths into and out of Porth-cadjack Cove.
❸ Reach car parking area above Basset's Cove. Follow broad track inland, then at public road, cross over and turn **R** for short distance.
❹ Turn **L** into car park. Go through car park and down tree-line track. Turn **L** at T-junction and follow track to another T-junction. There are private houses on other side of the junction. Turn **L** along broad track.
❺ Reach junction and 4-way signpost beside 2 seats. Keep straight on, signposted East Lodge. Reach junction by seat. Keep **R** and go through wooden kissing gate. Eyes **L** before crossing to check for golfers

about to tee-off. Go through kissing gate and continue to follow track alongside golf course.
❻ About 40yds (37m) beyond end of golf course section, at junction, bear off **L** into woods. Stay on main path, ignoring side paths, then bear round **R** to East Lodge car park and to public road.
❼ Cross road diagonally **R** and then go **L** between wooden posts with red marks. Keep to good track ahead. Pass holiday chalets and reach T-junction above farm buildings at Feadon Farm and Duchy College.
❽ Turn **L**; in few paces turn **R** down concrete track. At farmyard go sharp **L** by public footpath sign and follow path down through woods keeping to main path, to surfaced road. Just past 'Glenfeadon Castle' turn **L** along Glenfeadon Terrace, pass beneath bridge, then at junction keep ahead along Tregea Terrace and back to Portreath Beach car park.

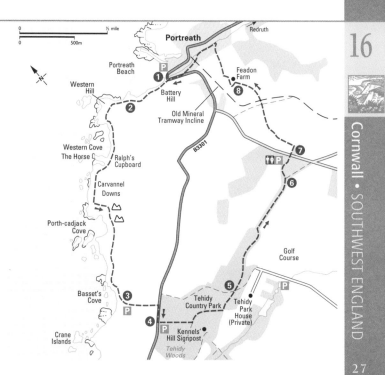

MULLION COVE Wildflower Haven

Wild flowers on the Lizard Peninsula heathland.

7 miles/11.3km 4hrs **Ascent** 164ft/50m ▲ **Difficulty** ☐1

Paths Good inland tracks and paths, can be muddy in places during wet weather. Coastal footpath, 21 stiles

Map OS Explorer 103 The Lizard **Grid ref** SW 669162 **Parking** Predannack Wollas Farm (NT)

❶ Leave bottom end of car park through gate by last house and follow track for 0.5 mile (800km). Where track bends **L** (signposted) continue on secondary track ahead to field gate in few steps. Beyond gate, keep ahead to cross stile in wall opposite just **L** of opening into field. Turn **L** along field edge. Cross stile; continue to open ground by gate in fence on **R**.

❷ Cross stile, then bear away from fence along path to English Nature's Kynance Farm Nature Reserve. Keep ahead towards distant buildings. At large field, keep along its **L** edge.

❸ In 100yds (92m), go **L** through gap, signposted, then cross next field to rough track. Turn **R** for few paces then go **L** through gate and turn **R**.

❹ Go through gate, then follow track **R**. Merge with another track, then in few paces, just before ford, bear off **R** along track towards coast.

❺ At crossing with coast path, go **R** and steeply uphill, then cross stile on to cliff top. Follow coast path round edge of cliffs at Pengersick and Vellan Head.

❻ Go **L** at junction, just past National Trust sign 'Predannack'. (Return to car park by following inland path from here.) Cross stream in dip and climb up **L** and continue along coast path to Mullion Cove and Harbour.

❼ Go up road from Mullion Harbour and just beyond public toilets and shop, turn off **R** at coast path sign. Keep to **R** of entrance to holiday site and follow track uphill. On bend, just before granite pillar, go **R** and over stone stile. Follow path ahead through thorn trees and then fields.

❽ Pass close to tall granite cross. Reach lane by houses. Keep ahead along lane towards Predannack Manor Farm. Just before farm entrance, go **L** over stile by field gate, then turn **R** along field edge. Cross stile, go **L** along hedged-in path, cross stile and cross 2 fields to lane (watch for traffic). Turn **R** to Predannack Wollas Farm car park.

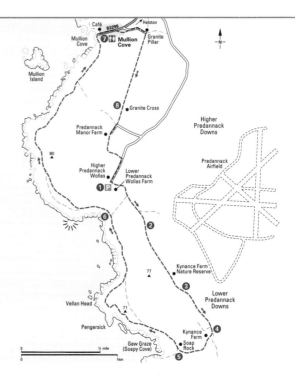

PRUSSIA COVE The Smuggler King
Through the domain of smuggler John Carter.

4 miles/6.4km 3hrs **Ascent** 394ft (120m) ⚠ **Difficulty** ☐1☐
Paths Good field paths and coastal paths, 18 stiles
Map OS Explorer 102 Land's End **Grid ref** SW 554282 **Parking** Trenalls, Prussia Cove. Small, privately owned car park. Or car park at Perranuthnoe, from where the walk can be started at Point ⑤

❶ From Trenalls car park entrance walk back along road, past large house. Keep **L** and round next sharp **R-H** bend. Watch for traffic. In 150yds (138m), just past field gate, walk through hidden gap **L** into field.
❷ Follow field edge, bearing **R** where it bends L, to stile by telegraph pole in hedge opposite. Walk down next field edge, behind Acton Castle (private). Turn **R**; follow bottom field edge to end. Cross stile; follow field edge to overgrown stile. Cross stile then, half-way along next field, go **L** over stile and turn **R** along lane.
❸ Turn **L** along rough track at junction in front of bungalow entrance at Trevean Farm. In 55yds (50m) by Trevean House keep **R**, up track; go through gate on **R**. Follow **L-H** edge of long field to stile in top edge. Follow R-H edge of next field.
❹ At Trebarvah cross stile and go through gate. Cross lane and continue across stony area with houses **R**, (St Michael's Mount ahead); follow field edge to hedged-in path. Follow path through fields; pass in front of houses to main road opposite Victoria Inn. Go **L** and

follow road to car park above Perranuthnoe Beach.
❺ Go **L**, just beyond car park, and along lane. Bear **R** at fork, then **R** again just past house at junction. Go down track towards sea and follow it round **L**. Then, at field entrance, go down **R** (signposted), turn sharp **L** through gap and follow track.
❻ At junction above Trevean Cove, bear off **R** from track and join path along cliff edge.
❼ At National Trust property of Cudden Point, follow path steeply uphill, then across inner slope of headland above Piskies Cove.
❽ Go through gate and pass fishing huts. Follow path round edge of Bessy's Cove inlet of Prussia Cove, and go up steps to track by cottage. Cove reached down path, **R**, just before this junction. Turn **R** and follow track, past post box. Keep **L** at junctions, to start.

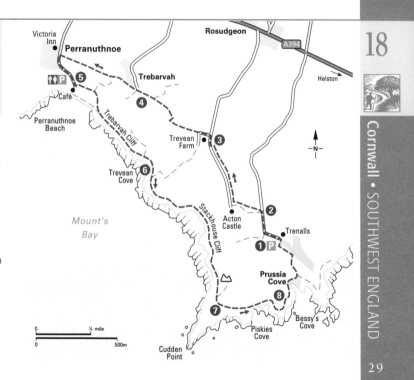

LAMORNA COVE Merry Maidens

A walk passing an ancient stone circle.

6 miles/9.7km 3hrs 30min **Ascent** 558ft/170m ⚠ **Difficulty** ☐2
Paths Good coastal footpaths, field paths and rocky tracks
Map OS Explorer 102 Land's End
Grid ref SW 450241 **Parking** Lamorna Cove or Boskena Cross

❶ From end of seaward car park above Lamorna Harbour, follow coast path. Continue along path past tops of Tregurnow Cliff and Rosemodress Cliff.
❷ Pass above entrance ramp and steps of Tater-du Lighthouse. Pass large residence on **R**; where track bends **R**, keep **L** along narrow coast path, at signpost.
❸ Descend steeply (take care if muddy) from Boscawen Cliff to St Loy's Cove. Cross over sea-smoothed boulders (slippery when wet). Mid-way along beach, follow path inland through trees and alongside stream. Cross private drive; climb steeply uphill. Go over stile on to track, turn **R** over stile and follow path through trees.
❹ By wooden signpost and old tree, go sharply down **R** and cross stream via boulders. Go **L** along hedged-in path. In 100yds (90m), go sharp **R** and up to surfaced lane. Follow lane uphill. At junction with track, keep ahead and uphill. At Boskenna Farm buildings follow surfaced lane round **L** and keep ahead.

❺ From lane, at entrance drive to bungalow on **R**, right of way goes through field gate, then diagonally **R** across field to wooden stile in wire fence. Beyond this, the way (no path) leads diagonally across field to top **R-H** corner, where stile leads into large roadside lay-by with granite cross at edge. Alternatively, continue from bungalow entrance along farm lane, then turn **R** along public road, with care, to reach lay-by.
❻ Follow road to Tregiffian burial chamber on **R** and then to Merry Maidens stone circle. From stone circle, follow grassy path to gate in field corner. Go over steep stile on **L**, turn **R** along field edge for 55yds (50m) and go **L** across field past telegraph pole. Cross stile on to road, go down **L-H** of 2 lanes, with 'No Through Road' sign.
❼ Where lane ends keep ahead on to public bridleway. Follow shady, rocky track (slippery when wet), downhill to public road. Turn **R**, walk down road with care, passing Lamorna Wink Inn, to car park.

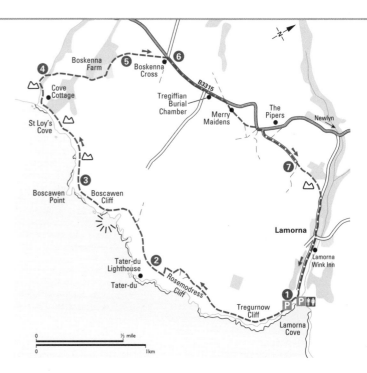

PORTHCURNO Golden Beaches And Cliff

Between sandy coves and granite cliffs on the Land's End peninsula.

3.5 miles/5.7km 2hrs 30min **Ascent** 164ft/50m ⚠ **Difficulty** 1️⃣
Paths Coastal footpaths
Map OS Explorer 102 Land's End **Grid ref** SW 384224
Parking Porthcurno, St Levan and Porthgwarra

1 From Porthcurno car park, walk back up approach road. Just before Sea View House, turn sharply **L** along track to cottages. Pass to **R** of cottages and turn **R** through gap. Follow field path past granite cross and go through wooden gate.

2 Enter St Levan churchyard by granite stile. Go round far side of church to entrance gate and on to surfaced lane. Cross lane and follow path opposite, signed 'Porthgwarra Cove'. Cross footbridge then in 55yds (50m), at junction, take **R** fork and follow path to merge with main coast path and keep ahead.

3 Where path begins to descend towards Porthgwarra Cove, branch off **R** up wooden steps. Reach surfaced track by house and turn up **R**, then at road, turn **L**.

4 Go round sharp **L-H** bend, then at footpath signpost, go **R** down grassy path and cross stone footbridge. Continue uphill to bend on track, just up from large granite houses.

5 Turn **L**, cross stile beside gate, then continue down surfaced lane to Porthgwarra Cove. Just past shop and café, and opposite red telephone box, go **R** down track, signposted Coast Path, then follow path round **L**. Just past house, go sharp **R** at junction and climb steps.

6 Continue along coast path, partly reversing previous route past Point **3**. Keep **R** at junction, and eventually descend past St Levan's Well to just above Porth Chapel Beach. (Dogs on leads.) Follow coast path steeply over Pedn-mên-an-mere, and continue to Minack Theatre car park.

7 If surefooted, cross car park and go down track to **L** of Minack complex, then descend steep cliff steps, with great care. When path levels off, continue to junction. The **R** fork leads to Porthcurno Beach and back to car park. Continuation leads to road opposite Beach Café, where **R** turn leads to car park. For less challenging alternative to cliff steps, turn **L** out of Minack car park. Follow approach road to T-junction with public road. Turn **R**, watching for traffic.

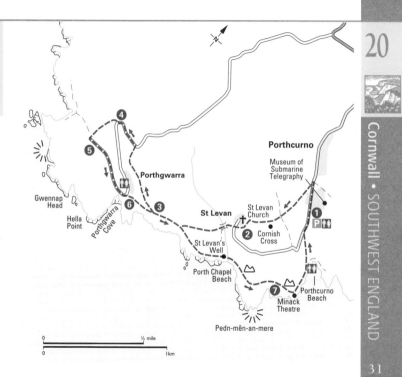

21

COLYTON The River Coly And The Umborne Brook

Along the River Coly and Umborne Brook.

4.25 miles/6.8km 2hrs 30min **Ascent** 197ft/60m ⚠ **Difficulty** 2

Paths Fields and lanes, parts boggy after wet weather, 7 stiles

Map OS Explorer 116 Lyme Regis & Bridport **Grid ref** SY 246940

Parking Paying car park in centre of Colyton (Dolphin Street)

Devon · SOUTHWEST ENGLAND

❶ Turn **R**, then 1st **L** into Lower Church Street. **L** at Gerrard Arms into Rosemary Lane; **R** into Vicarage Street. Go **R**, towards river, cross bridge.

❷ Turn **L** through kissing gate and along river bank on East Devon Way (EDW). Continue through 2 kissing gates. Ignore next footpath sign **R**; keep ahead through kissing gate, over stream, and through gate.

❸ Keep along riverbank; at footpath junction at field end take kissing gate in corner ahead on to concrete walkway. Go through kissing gate, cross field, aiming for kissing gate/footbridge under 3 big oaks. Keep ahead, cross footbridge/gate to bridge over river, **L**.

❹ Turn **R** (leaving EDW), to gate on to lane, turn **R**. At Cadhayne Farm (**R**) turn **L** through gate opposite farmyard. Walk up field, through gate at top and straight on. Green lane bears sharp **L**; turn **R** along muddy track, ending at road signed 'Tritchayne'.

❺ Cross, walk downhill along Watery Lane. After Tritchmarsh follow footpath sign **R** on walkway. Go

sharp **L** to gate and **L** round field. Ignore next stile **L**; take next small gate/bridge/gate and cross paddock and Umborne Brook via gate and concrete walkway to Lexhayne Mill. Continue between house and yard to kissing gate; go over stile in wire fence (railway ahead). Cross next stile; head diagonally **R** for Lexhayne Farm drive. Cross stile, keep ahead through hedge gap.

❻ Cross field diagonally to bottom corner, over double gate/bridge and footbridge over brook. Walk **L**; over stile, keep ahead to cross brook via footbridge/double gate with Colyton church ahead.

❼ Aim for stile in fence ahead **R**. Bear diagonally **L** to cross brook via double gate/bridge, then **L**. Cross stile and 2 stiles/footbridges then diagonally across upper part of next field. Descend and cross stile to road.

❽ Turn **L**; pass picnic area/playground at Road Green, then over bridge. Take 1st **L** (Vicarage Street), go straight on to pass church (**L**), through town centre and down Silver Street to car park.

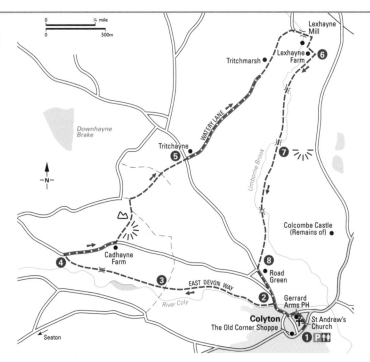

32

BROADHEMBURY An Unspoiled Village

Beech woods and rolling farmland around an unspoiled thatched village.

5.75 miles/9.2km 2hrs 30min **Ascent** 360ft/110m ⚠ **Difficulty** 2
Paths Country lanes, pastures and woodland paths, 7 stiles
Map OS Explorer 115 Exeter & Sidmouth **Grid ref** SY 096069
Parking Unsurfaced car park at Rhododendron Wood

❶ Return to road and turn **L** uphill. Soon bridleway sign points **R** through parking area. Follow path along airfield perimeter, eventually climbing to wooden gate.
❷ Go though gate and turn **R** along edge of airfield, eventually keeping to **R** of clubhouse. Follow tarmac drive **R** over cattle grid and keep ahead to join road.
❸ Turn **R**; pass Barleycombe Farm (**L**), then follow bridleway signs **R** through gate, downhill then **L** through another and into field. Walk along bottom of field. Path curves **R** through stand of beech trees and metal gate, then runs straight across next field towards big beech tree and gate. Take stony track through gate. Keeping fence on **R** walk on to pass through gate, with coniferous plantation to **R**.
❹ Path ends at lane; turn **R** downhill into Broadhembury. At St Andrew's Church cross road and go through churchyard (no dogs), then under lychgate and downhill to find The Drewe Arms (**L**).
❺ To continue walk, from pub, turn **L** down main street to reach bridge and ford. Turn **R** up lane, past

playground and up hill, eventually bearing **R**.
❻ Just past 2 thatched cottages (**R**) go **L** over stile in hedge and up field, aiming for stile in top **L** corner. Go over that and straight ahead, passing to **L** of farmhouse and barn conversions. Over next stile; round next, then cross another; then **R**, round edge of field, and over two small stiles into small copse. Another stile leads into next field; bear slightly **R** to locate next stile in beech hedge opposite, which takes you into green lane.
❼ Turn **R** and walk uphill with conifers **L** and fields **R** until metal gate leads to another and back on to airfield.
❽ Turn **L** along edge of field. Follow bridleway **L** through 1st gate, and continue back to road. Turn **L** downhill to find your car.

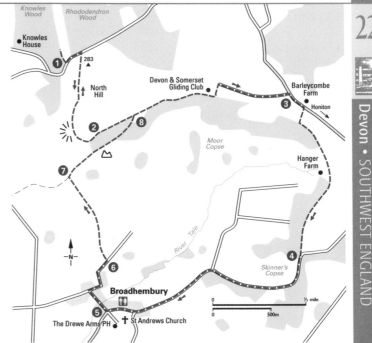

BICKLEIGH The Exe Valley Way

Leave the crowds behind at Bickleigh Bridge and explore the quiet lanes of the lovely Exe Valley.

5.75 miles/9.2km 2hrs 15min **Ascent** 509ft/155m ⚠ **Difficulty** ⊡2

Paths Country lanes, one long, steep track
Map OS Explorer 114 Exeter & the Exe Valley **Grid ref** SX 938075
Parking Laneside near railway bridge at Bickleigh Mill, off A396

❶ From laneside near Bickleigh Mill go back, with care, to A396 and cross bridge. Turn **L** down A3072, following brown tourist sign for Bickleigh Castle. Take first lane **L**, running along edge of flood plain on Exe Valley Way (EVW). Bickleigh Castle will soon be found on R. Go straight on along lane.

❷ Pass Way Farm and take next lane **R** to leave Exe Valley Way, roughly signposted 'Lee Cross & Perry Farm'. Take care, this is very narrow lane, carrying traffic from local farms. Keep along lane as it climbs steeply uphill and after 700yds (640m) brings you to farm at Lee Cross. Keep ahead up lane to pass Perry Lodge. Eventually lane bears sharp **L** and then R.

❸ Turn **L** on green lane and walk uphill. Pass restored chapel – St Martins – on **L**, and keep ahead; at last track levels off.

❹ Where green lane meets tarmac lane turn **L** and proceed steeply downhill (EVW). Glorious views over River Exe, and to Silverton church beyond. Follow lane down until you see Tray Mill Farm on R.

❺ Way home is straight on, but it's worth making a short detour to river here. Turn **R** through farmyard and pass through metal gate on to concrete standing. Cross field, aiming for suspension bridge ahead. Cross over (not for faint-hearted!) to reach dismantled railway track. Do not turn **L** along track – although it would take you back to your car– it is privately owned and has no public right of way.

❻ Path goes straight on here to meet A369. You can do that, turn L, then eventually **R** to walk through Bickleigh village to mill, but road is busy and you would be better advised to retrace your steps to Tray Mill Farm and take quieter route back to Bickleigh Mill.

❼ Back on lane by Tray Mill Farm, turn **R** and walk straight along lane, past Bickleigh Castle, turning **R** at A3072, and **R** again over bridge to return to car.

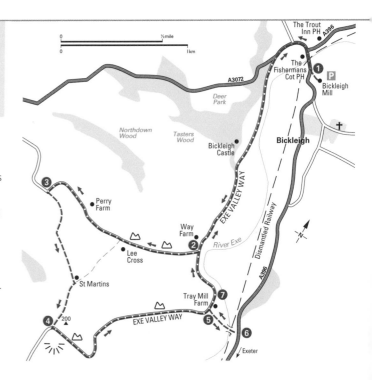

OTTERTON Birdlife At The Reserve

Along the River Otter towards High Peak.

4.25 miles/6.8km 2hrs **Ascent** 164ft/50m ⚠ **Difficulty** ☐ 1

Paths Good level paths, coastal section and lanes, 1 stile
Map OS Explorer 115 Exeter & Sidmouth **Grid ref** SX 076831
Parking By side of broad, quiet lane near entrance to South Farm

❶ Walk through kissing gate to **R** of South Farm gate. Turn **R** following signs for 'Coast Path Ladram Bay'. Narrow, sandy path runs along field edge.

❷ At end of field shallow flight of wooden steps leads to walkway and footbridge, and up into next field. There are good views downriver to shingle bank at Budleigh Salterton and across river to cricket pitch.

❸ Path continues gently downhill until it turns sharply **L** following line of coast. Just before you turn east there are panoramic views **R** over Otter delta, and along beach.

❹ After just over 1 mile (1.6km) path rises and view of Lyme Bay opens up ahead, including High Peak 564ft/157m (one of highest points on South Devon coast). Follow coast path: red sandstone cliffs are extremely friable and 'chunks' continually tumble seawards, but path is safe. Pass through small gate by disused outlook building (covered bench), and continue downhill.

❺ Turn **L** to leave coast path on 'Permissive path to

Otterton'; this narrow, grassy path goes through kissing gate; turn immediately **L** and follow path **R** around water treatment works, and up gravelly lane to meet Stantyway Road. Turn **L** up track, which soon bears **R**, signed to River Otter, and gives way to tarmac lane.

❻ After 400yds (366m) Clamour Bridge is signed to **L**. Turn **L** here and follow narrow, wooded green lane, which ends at gate. Go through, then almost immediately another, and follow signs along edge of next field, to leave over stile on to track.

❼ Turn immediately **L** between 2 big ornamental brick pillars, and **R** under very large oak tree. Descend short flight of steps and cross over River Otter on Clamour Bridge.

❽ Turn **L**, follow river south; over small leat (look for aqueduct coming across meadows on **R**), through kissing gate and continue to White Bridge, where you go through kissing gate, turn **L** and your car.

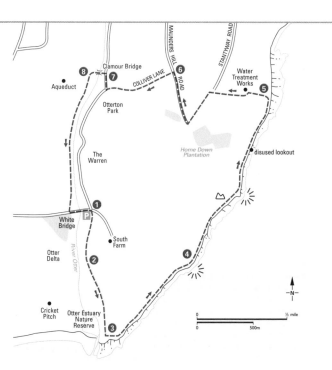

KILLERTON The National Trust
Around the beautiful Killerton Estate.

4.25 miles/6.8km 2hrs 15min **Ascent** 131ft/40m ⚠ **Difficulty** 1

Paths Good footpaths, bridleways and farm tracks, 4 stiles

Map OS Explorer 114 Exeter & the Exe Valley **Grid ref** SX 977002

Parking National Trust car park plus overflow car park

❶ From car park return to road and turn **R** to reach gate and cattle grid at entrance drive to Killerton House. Follow public footpath sign towards house, passing stables and courtyard on **R** from where ticket holders approach house.

❷ Bear **L** off drive at house entrance, across grass. Pass to **L** of house and continue straight on, past walled gardens and ornamental lawns. Soon pass through kissing gate in hedge ahead into sloping field.

❸ Turn **R** uphill, keeping by hedge and then metal fence on **R**. At top of field ignore public footpath sign 'Bluebell Gate', and turn **L** down across field to enter Columbjohn Wood through small gate.

❹ Turn **L**, and immediately branch **L** again on higher path round wooden barrier, which leads gradually downhill. Leave wood by kissing gate, and keep straight on to meet and follow farm track. After 250yds (229m) cross stile on **R** to enter field. Keeping wood on your **R**, pass cottage to arrive at 16th-century Columbjohn Chapel.

❺ Cross stile to gain grassy drive on other side of chapel, and look **L** at old gatehouse archway. Retrace steps through field back to farm track.

❻ Turn **L** and follow level track through woods and fields around edge of estate. River Culm on **L**, but you will be more aware of main Penzance-to-Paddington railway. Track reaches road by Ellerhayes Bridge.

❼ Ignore road; turn **R** to follow edge of parkland and woods, keeping road on your **L**. Pass through several gates on NT bridlepath, which eventually goes through 2 gates to join gravel track. Turn **L** downhill to pass entrance to Chapel of the Holy Evangelists, built in Norman style in 1842 for Aclands, their tenants and employees, and to replace one at Columbjohn.

❽ Continue on to meet road. Turn **R** downhill, then **R** at junction, and **R** again into car park.

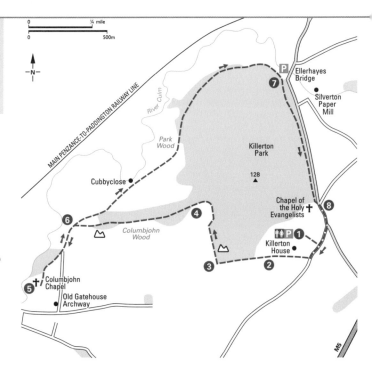

WITHLEIGH Watching For Buzzards

A walk through peaceful hillside woods and along river banks.

3.5 miles/5.7k 2hrs **Ascent** 150ft/45m ⚠ **Difficulty** 1
Paths Waymarked paths, tracks (some muddy) and quiet lanes, 2 stiles
Map OS Explorer 114 Exeter & the Exe Valley **Grid ref** SX 905121 **Parking** A narrow lane (No Through Road) leads to NT Buzzards car park from B3137 near sign to parish church

❶ Cross stile into field, and turn **R**. At hedge ahead bear **L** and walk to wood. Descend steeply at wood edge, heading for gate and stone water trough.
❷ Once through gate go straight ahead, keeping hedge **L**. Go through gate and continue with tiny River Dart on **R**. Before bridge turn **L** at waymarker, through small gate into field. Turn **R**, keeping high hedge **R**.
❸ Leave field through next gate, which leads on to broad track which rises through Cross's Wood. Soon after passing bench, waymarker directs you **L**, off track and back into woods up fairly steep path, which can be muddy in places. Continue to climb until path reaches wide track at top of woods.
❹ Turn **R** to follow track gently downhill, through gate into open area where it zig-zags more steeply downhill between gorse, broom and bracken.
❺ Pass Buzzards Cottage and follow track **L** to join riverside track. Follow track ahead; before bridge over river (**R**), turn **L** on broad track. After few paces turn **R** over stile and plank bridge to enter field.

❻ Keep hedge on **L** and walk through field for 250yds (229m) to gate into Huntland Wood. Follow path steeply uphill. Eventually join track; bear **R**. Track levels off and leads through beautiful upper wood before descending gradually to leave wood at lane.
❼ Turn **R** downhill, cross Dart at Worthy Bridge, turn **R** at next junction (signed 'Cruwys Morchard'), eventually passing Thongsleigh Mill (**R**). Where lane bends **L**, go straight ahead through gate on to track. Where this drops to river keep ahead, eventually passing through gate and into Thongsleigh Wood.
❽ Continue along track, with river, **R**. At big gate leave wood and enter meadows; path here is faint but continues straight ahead. Next metal gate leads on to lane. Turn **R** over Groubear Bridge and climb back up ancient rocky lane to car park.

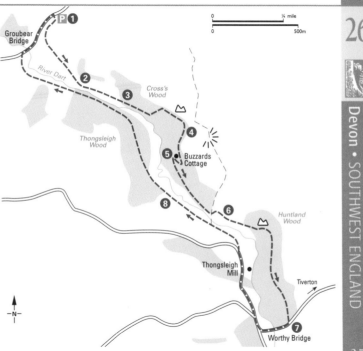

Devon • SOUTHWEST ENGLAND

27

Devon • SOUTHWEST ENGLAND

BRAMPFORD SPEKE The Meandering Exe
Water-meadows, ox-bow lakes and herons.

3.5 miles/5.7km 1hr 30min **Ascent** Negligible ⚠ **Difficulty** 1
Paths Grassy field paths, tracks and country lanes, 2 stiles **Map** OS Explorer 114 Exeter & the Exe Valley
Grid ref SX 927982 **Parking** On laneside near St Peter's Church, Brampford Speke

❶ Follow Exe Valley Way (EWW) footpath signs down lane to **R** of church, then **L** through churchyard. Leave via metal gate, and follow path on through kissing gate. Meet lane at wooden kissing gate under lychgate.
❷ Turn **R** and follow footpath signs downhill to cross River Exe over large wooden bridge. Bear **L** across meadow, following footpath signs. Note old station and stationmaster's house (private) on **R**. Ignore footpath sign pointing **R** and go through gateway in hedge ahead; keep close to river (**L**).
❸ Follow river around flood plain. Cross old rail line via 2 kissing gates. **L** are railway bridge piers in river.
❹ Immediately through 2nd gate drop down **L** to river and continue straight on. Cross stile and keep ahead to pass through double kissing gate, then later cross another stile.
❺ Follow river; after 1 mile (1.6km) path bears **R** away from river down track to kissing gate. Turn immediately **L** along another track. At next footpath

post go straight on (ignoring EWW signs **L**) along green lane. Hedges disappear and lane crosses arable farmland, ending at road on edge of Rewe.
❻ Turn **R** along lane towards Stoke Canon to pass old cross at Burrow Farm. Carry straight on to pass Oakhay Barton. Note Stoke Canon level crossing on Exeter–Tiverton line ahead.
❼ Before level crossing follow footpath sign **R** through kissing gate and along fenced path. Pass through next kissing gate and metal gate to join dismantled railway line. Pass through kissing gate; go straight on. River Exe loops in on **L** and Brampford Speke church is ahead above river. Kissing gate leads over small bridge and into copse. Another kissing gate leads back into meadows (marshy in winter, but there is small wooden footbridge, **R**, for use at such times) and to footbridge over Exe.
❽ Once over the, retrace steps up path, turning **L** at lychgate and back through churchyard to your car.

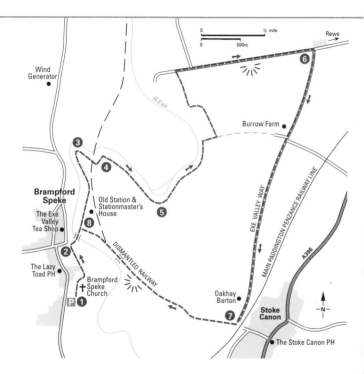

38

STEPS BRIDGE A Dartmoor Outlier

A climb up Heltor Rock and a church.

5 miles/8km 2hrs 45min **Ascent** 393ft/120m ⚠ **Difficulty** 2
Paths Woodland paths, open fields and country lanes, 3 stiles **Map** OS Explorer 110 Torquay
& Dawlish **Grid ref** SX 803884 **Parking** Free car park (and tourist information board) at Steps Bridge

❶ Cross road, following signs to former youth hostel. Turn **R** up track, then **L** as signed towards building; path bears **R**, ('Heltor Farm'). Steep path leads uphill through woodland. At top of wood cross ladder stile.
❷ Follow wooden footpath posts straight up field and through gate. Keep up **L** edge of next field; pass through gateway and look **L** for Heltor Rock.
❸ At end of field turn **L** as signed through gate into plantation; follow path to meet gate to lane. Turn **L**, walk uphill to tarmac lane.
❹ Turn **L** (' Bridford'). After 200yds (183m) turn **L** over stile up narrow fenced permissive path to Heltor, for panorama. Retrace steps to road and turn **L**.
❺ After 1 mile (1.6km) lane bears **L**, then **R**, to edge of Bridford. Turn **R** ('Parish Hall & Church'). Follow church wall path, down steps and **R** to Bridford Inn.
❻ Turn **L** and follow lane through village. Take 4th turning (Neadon Lane) on **R**, by telephone box. Just past where bridleway joins (from **L**) lane dips **R**, downhill; take **L** fork ahead to pass Birch Down Farm

on **R**. Keep straight on at Westbirch Farm; turn **L** signed 'Lowton Farm' on fenced path, which bears **R** to kissing gate; pass through and up **R** next field edge to stile in top corner. Cross tumbledown wall and carry on through gorse bushes. Cross stile by beech trees.
❼ Follow fenced path along top of 2 fields, and down green lane to Lower Lowton Farm. Turn **R** as signed before farm on permissive bridlepath, which descends (stream, **R**) then rises to signpost; turn **R** for Steps Bridge down green lane, pass through gate. Continue down green lane to reach surfaced lane though gate.
❽ Turn **L** through middle gate, ('Byway to Steps Bridge'). At edge of Bridford Wood (by NT sign) turn **R** following footpath signposts. Path is narrow and steep. Go **L**, then **R**, to cross track, downhill. Path drops down steps then runs to **L**, now high above river to Steps Bridge where it meets road opposite former café. Turn **L** to return to car.

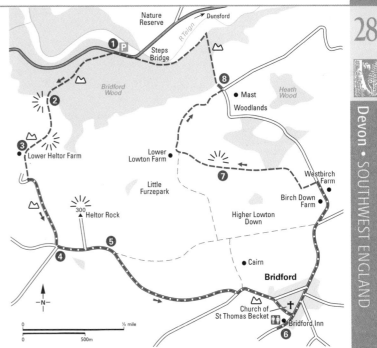

LUSTLEIGH Wooded Bovey Valley
Exploring wooded Bovey Valley.

4.75 miles/7.7km 2hrs 30min **Ascent** 754ft/230m ▲ **Difficulty** ③
Paths Steep rocky ascents/descents, rough paths and woodland
Map OS Explorer OL28 Dartmoor
Grid ref SX 775816 **Parking** By side of lane at Hammerslake

❶ From parking area walk north up lane (away from Lustleigh) and turn **L** up narrow rocky path between houses 'Logan Stones' and 'Grove', signed 'Cleave for Water'. At gate go straight ahead signed 'Hunters Tor' and climb steeply up to top (views to Hound Tor).

❷ Turn **R** through woodland; reach open ground and follow path straight on over highest part of ridge and across remains of Iron Age fort to reach Hunter's Tor.

❸ Pass through gate **R** of tor and follow signed path **R** down to signed path **L**. Walk down through gate, then **R** through another and down to Peck Farm. Go through gate **L** of farm and on down concrete drive.

❹ Shortly after turn **L** through gate signed 'Foxworthy Bridge' and continue along wooded track to Foxworthy; turn **R**.

❺ At path junction go **L**, signed 'Horsham'. Follow track into woodland through gate. After 5 minutes follow signs **R** for 'Horsham for Manaton & Water', to River Bovey. Follow river bank **L** for few paces to crossing (on boulders) at Horsham Steps. To avoid crossing Horsham Steps, don't turn **L** for 'Horsham' at Point ❺, go **R**, down drive, which crosses the river. Take the 1st footpath **L** and keep ahead to rejoin main route at Point ❻; turn **R** uphill.

❻ Cross, taking care, and walk downstream to enter Bovey Valley Woodlands. Follow path steeply uphill (path avoiding Horsham Steps comes in **R**) and over stile. Keep ahead to pass through gate by cottages (note tree-branch porch). Keep on up track, following signs for 'Water' through Letchole Plantation.

❼ At track crossroads turn **R** ('Manaton direct') to lane by Water Mill. Take the 2nd lane **R** to Kestor Inn.

❽ Return to crossroads. Descend, signed 'Bovey Valley', to split in track. Keep **L**, eventually passing through gate and down steep path. Cross river on bridge and proceed steeply uphill to signpost. Go **L**, signed 'Lustleigh via Hammerslake', and **L** again at next signpost (steep). At junction keep ahead uphill; where path forks keep **R** to gate; turn **R** down rocky path back to lane at start.

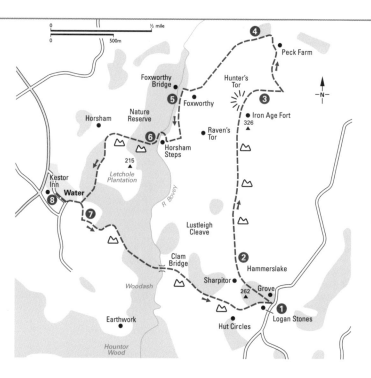

BOVEY TRACEY Dartmoor's National Park
Woodlands and an old railway line.

3 miles/4.8km 1hr 30min **Ascent** 196ft/60m ⚠ **Difficulty** ☐1

Paths Woodland and field paths, some muddy, 2 stiles
Map OS Explorer 110 Torquay & Dawlish **Grid ref** SX 814782
Parking Car park on the B3344 at lower end of Fore Street, Bovey Tracey

① Cross road and turn **R**, following signs 'Town centre shops'. Just before bridge turn **L** along concrete walkway into Mill Marsh Park, past children's playground and through arboretum. Level footpath leads past sports field to busy A382 at Hole Bridge via kissing gate. Cross road carefully.
② Enter kissing gate and turn **R** to enter NT's Parke Estate on trackbed of dismantle Newton Abbot-to-Moretonhampstead railway. Follow path over river.
③ Turn immediately **L** down wooden steps and through kissing gate to follow river. Cross stile at field end and continue on narrow, rough path, high above river. Descend steps; cross footbridge into next field.
④ Parke is over bridge to **L**; old railway line is **R**, but keep ahead through field into woodland, then go **L** on raised wooden walkway to river. Path winds on, then runs between woods with fields on **R**, then over footbridge to river at weir. Keep following river; eventually 2 kissing gates lead out of NT land. Keep ahead to pass footbridge over river. Later, bear **R** to

cross railway track. Turn half **L** down to lane via gate.
⑤ Turn **L** (signed 'Manaton') and pass between old railway bridge piers. Walk across Wilford Bridge, ignoring signs to Lustleigh, **R**. Continue up lane past Forder gatehouses, **R**, then go steeply uphill until lane bends sharp **R**.
⑥ Turn **L** over stile to re-enter Parke Estate. Wooded path is narrow. Go through wood and kissing gate to large field. Keep to **R**, dropping downhill, to leave via kissing gate and wooded path parallel to road.
⑦ Path ends at kissing gate; turn sharp **L**; cross parkland and drive to Parke car park. Go down to cross lower drive, then **L** to go below house, ending at 5-bar gate. Enter; turn **R** ('Riverside Walk') to cross river at Parke Bridge, then ahead to join old railway track.
⑧ Turn **R** and follow track until it crosses the Bovey, to meet A382. Cross road to enter Mill Marsh Park and retrace steps to your car.

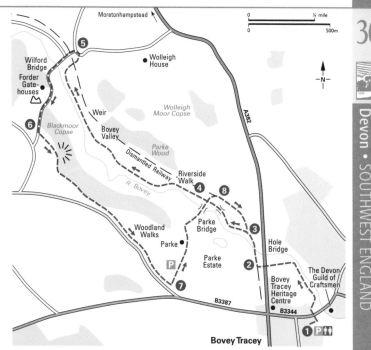

DARTINGTON A Medieval Mansion
Around the Dartington Hall Estate.

6.5 miles/10.4km 2hrs 30min **Ascent** 164ft/50m ⚠ **Difficulty** 1
Paths Fields, woodland tracks and country lanes, 4 stiles **Map** OS Explorer 110 Torquay & Dawlish
Grid ref SX 799628 **Parking** Opposite entrance to Dartington Hall **Note** Larger organised groups require permission from the Property Administrator (01803 847000) in advance

❶ Turn **L** downhill. Follow pavement to River Dart.
❷ Turn **L** through gate (no footpath sign) and follow river northwards. This part of walk is likely to be very muddy after rainfall. River Dart here is broad, tree-lined and slow-moving. Pass through 1 gate, then another, through woodland and gate. Continue through riverside meadows, and eventually pass through open gateway on to wooded track.
❸ Walk along river edge of next field (Park Copse **L**). At end of field gate leads into Staverton Ford Plantation. Where track bears **L** go through gate in wall ahead, then **R** on narrow path towards river, bearing **L** over footbridge. Path runs parallel with Dart, becoming broad woodland track through North Wood. When buildings appear through trees on **R**, leave track and walk downhill to metal gate and lane.
❹ Turn **R** to cross Staverton Bridge. At level crossing turn **R**; pass through Staverton Station yard into park-like area between railway and river. Follow path across

railway and meet lane by Sweet William Cottage.
❺ Turn **R** and follow lane to its end. Go straight ahead on small gritty path to pass Church of St Paul de Leon, who was 9th-century travelling preacher. Turn **L** at lane to pass public toilets, and **L** at junction to Sea Trout Inn. After your break retrace steps to metal gate past Staverton Bridge.
❻ Turn immediately **R** to rejoin track. Follow this until it runs downhill and bends **L**. Walk towards gate on **R**, then turn **L** on narrow concrete path. Houses of Huxham's Cross can be seen, **R**. Keep on concrete path, which leaves woodland to run between wire fences to meet concrete drive at Dartington Crafts Education Centre. Follow drive to road.
❼ Turn **L** to pass Old Parsonage Farm. Keep on road back to Dartington Hall, passing gardens and ruins of the original church (**R**), until you see car park on **L**.

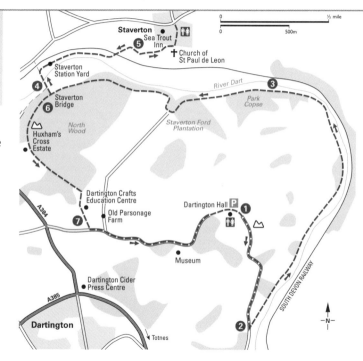

COLETON FISHACRE Wartime Secrets

The delights of Coleton Fishacre.

4.75 miles/7.7km 3hrs **Ascent** 525ft/160m ▲ **Difficulty** ③
Paths Varying coast path, tracks and lanes, steep steps, 7 stiles
Map OS Explorer OL20 South Devon **Grid ref** SX 910512
Parking National Trust car park at Coleton Camp

❶ Walk through kissing gate in top **R** corner of car park to take permissive path towards metal gate and stile ('link path to Ivy Cove'). Keeping hedge **R** walk downhill to cross 3 stiles at bottom of field. Bear **L** to next stile. Continue uphill to coast path (signs to Pudcombe Cove, **R**).

❷ Turn **R** and follow path along cliff. Eventually go through gate and descend steeply and over footbridge to reach gate at bottom of Coleton Fishacre gardens (no public right of way into gardens here).

❸ Turn **L**, following coast path signs, to pass steps to cove and go very steeply up steps to leave estate via gate and on to Coleton Cliffs. Path drops steeply, then climbs again above Old Mill Bay – with great views of the Mew Stone – followed by steep climb up to Outer Froward Point, with views towards Start Point. Path undulates, then climbs steeply to back of Froward Cove. Follow coast path signs **L** for Kingswear.

❹ Pass through gate, then follow coast path signs **L**, very steeply downhill through wooded section. Path

undulates towards Inner Froward Point.

❺ Look-out (once housing searchlight) is next landmark, followed by 104 steps up cliff. Follow miniature railway line uphill and keep to walkway and steps to pass through disused wartime buildings. At top is junction of paths and wooden footpath sign.

❻ Turn **L** for Kingswear to walk through woodland behind Newfoundland Cove, through gate and eventually a V-stile, and down woodland track (estuary **L**). Descend 84 steps to Mill Bay Cove and turn **R** down tarmac way. Turn **L** over stile and climb 89 steps up to lane, then 63 steps to another lane.

❼ Turn **R** ('Brownstone'). After 250yds (229m) lane forks; take **R** fork downhill to Home Cottage.

❽ Follow footpath signs, **R** up steep, rocky path to concrete lane, and on to pass Higher Brownstone Farm. Walk on up lane to pass NT car park, then gates to Coleton Fishacre, and back to car park.

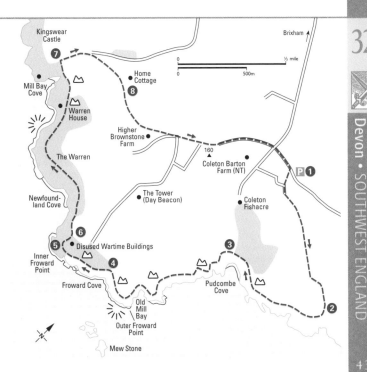

SOUTHWEST ENGLAND • Devon

33

DARTMOUTH A Port And A Castle
Along the cliffs to Dartmouth Castle.

3.5 miles/5.7km 2hrs **Ascent** 115ft/35m ⚠ **Difficulty** 1
Paths Easy coastal footpath and green lanes, 1 stile
Map OS Explorer OL20 South Devon **Grid ref** SX 874491
Parking National Trust car parks at Little Dartmouth

❶ Car parks at Little Dartmouth are signposted off B3205 (from A379 Dartmouth-to-Stoke Fleming road). Go through **R-H** car park, following signs 'Coast Path Dartmouth'. Continue through kissing gate, keeping hedge to your **R**. Walk through next field, through gate and kissing gate to join coast path.

❷ Turn **L**. Coast path runs little inland from cliff edge, but you can walk out on to Warren Point (plaque reveals that Devon Federation of Women's Institutes gave this land to National Trust in 1970).

❸ From Warren Point follow coast to pass above Western Combe Cove (steps down to sea) and then Combe Point (take care of long drop to sea from here).

❹ Rejoin coast path through open gateway in wall and follow it above Shinglehill Cove. Path turns inland, passes pond and follows track, then bears **R** along back of Willow Cove. It passes above woods (field **L**) and climbs to pass through gate. Follow yellow arrow

ahead to reach footpath post, then turn sharp **R** down valley, bearing **R** at bottom to stile as signed. Follow path on, and through gate near Compass Cove.

❺ Follow coast path **L** over footbridge, and continue towards Blackstone Point. Path turns inland to run along side of estuary through deciduous woodland.

❻ Path meets surfaced lane opposite Compass Cottage; keep ahead on to lane and immediately **R** again steeply downhill. Follow coast path signs **R** to zig-zag steeply down then up steps to reach turning space, then go **R** down steps to reach castle and café.

❼ Retrace your route up steps, then turn **L** up lane to Point ❻, then **L** to pass Compass Cottage, and continue straight on up steep lane (signposted 'Little Dartmouth') and through kissing gate on to National Trust land.

❽ Path runs along field top and through 5-bar gate on to green lane. Go through gate and farmyard at Little Dartmouth and ahead on lane to car park.

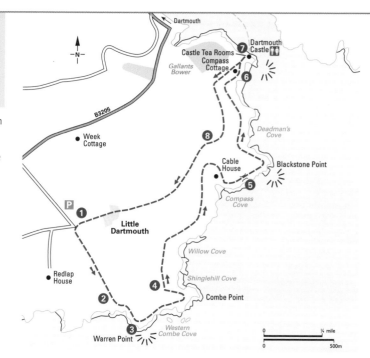

44

EAST PRAWLE The Deep South

A land of shipwrecks and smugglers, gannets and skuas.

4 miles/6.4km 2hrs **Ascent** 394ft/120m ⚠ **Difficulty** 2
Paths Green lanes, fields and coast path, rocky in places, 2 stiles
Map OS Explorer OL20 South Devon **Grid ref** SX 780363
Parking Around green in East Prawle (honesty box contributions)

1 Walk down lane towards sea, leaving green **L** and toilets and phone box **R** and following sign 'Prawle Point'. After few minutes lane turns sharp **L**; go straight ahead along rutted lane marked 'Public Bridleway'.
2 Green lane ends at T-junction (metal gates opposite); turn **L** down narrow grassy path between tumbledown walls. Follow path through kissing gate to footpath post.
3 Turn **R** downhill to coast path high above secluded Maceley Cove, with Gammon Head to **R**. Turn **L** and walk along path above Elender Cove. There is steep, scrambly access to both beaches but take care.
4 Path leads through kissing gate and scrambles on around Signalhouse Point. Steep ascent, partly stepped, is rewarded with fine views ahead to wreck of Demetrios on rocks, with Prawle Point beyond. Follow footpath posts through gate and across grassy down, keeping to **R** of coastguard lookout ahead.
5 At coastguard lookout enjoy superb views east to Lannacombe, Mattiscombe Sand and Start Point.

Explore excellent visitor centre, which will tell you everything you want to know about area. To continue, follow grassy path inland, rejoining coast path, and head towards old coastguard cottages.
6 Turn **R** through kissing gate to pass in front of cottages and along edge of level, grassy wavecut platform which lies just below original Pleistocene cliffs here. Pass through gate (note parking area across field to **L**) and along lovely level meadows above low cliffs. Go through next kissing gate. Next gate leads on to Langerstone Point. Continue round field edges and through another gate; Maelcombe House is now in sight ahead. Pass through 2 more gates and keep ahead to path junction.
7 Turn **L** up bridleway; eventually pass through gate and keep ahead up track.
8 Take 1st stile **R** to go steeply up field. Cross stone stile at top and continue **R** up narrow rocky track to join lane, ascending **R** steeply back to village.

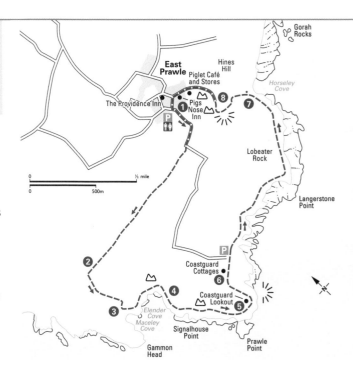

EAST PORTLEMOUTH Kingsbridge Estuary

A stroll around sleepy East Portlemouth.

4 miles/6.4km 2hrs **Ascent** 377ft/115m ⚠ **Difficulty** 2

Paths Good coast path, field paths and tracks

Map OS Explorer OL20 South Devon **Grid ref** SX 746386

Parking Near phone box in East Portlemouth or in small parking area

1 Park on the verge near phone box at East Portlemouth (or in parking area – village hall fund contributions). Go across parking area and steeply downhill on narrow tarmac footpath signposted 'Salcombe', which gives way to steep steps.

2 At lane at bottom of steps, turn **R** to visit The Venus Café and catch ferry to Salcombe. If you want to get on with walk, turn **L** along lane as it follows edge of estuary. This is official route of coast path and it passes some very exclusive residences.

3 Lane leads to pretty, sandy beach at Mill Bay. Carefully follow acorn coast path signs for Gara Rock through sycamore wood, with lovely views across estuary, and glimpses of inviting little coves.

4 At Limebury Point you reach open cliff, from where there are great views to South Sands and Overbecks opposite and craggy Bolt Head. Coast path now bears eastwards below Portlemouth Down, which was divided into strip fields in late 19th century.

5 Path along this stretch undulates steeply, and is rocky in places. Keep going until you reach bench and viewpoint over beach at Rickham Sands. Just beyond this, as coast path continues **R** (access to beach), take **L** fork and climb steeply below lookout to signpost by site of old Gara Rock Hotel (demolished 2006).

6 Turn **L** to hotel drive and walk straight on up lane. After 250yds (229m) turn **L** through gate in hedge signposted 'Mill Bay'. Walk ahead through gate and across field, bearing **R** to gate. Go through small copse, then gate and across farm track. Go through gate down public bridleway.

7 This runs gradually downhill beneath huge, ancient, pollarded lime trees, with grassy combe to **R**. Path leads past car park to reach Mill Bay.

8 Turn **R** along lane. If you want to avoid steps, look out for footpath sign pointing **R**, up narrow, steep, path to regain East Portlemouth and your car; if not, continue along lane and retrace your route up steps.

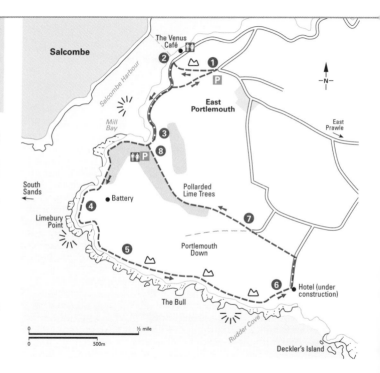

KINGSTON Peace And Solitude

A magical part of the county's south coast that even those who live in Devon seldom manage to find.

5.5 miles/8.8km 2hrs 30min **Ascent** 394ft/120m ⚠ **Difficulty** ③
Paths Fields, tracks and good coast path, 6 stiles
Map OS Explorer OL20 South Devon **Grid ref** SX 635478
Parking By St James the Less Church in Kingston village

❶ With church **L**, follow lane up to Wonwell Gate and turn **R** down lane signed 'Wonwell Beach'. When it bends sharp **R** then **L**, turn **L** through hedge gap and straight on, keeping hedge **L**. Pass through hedge into next field, then follow sign **R**, diagonally across field. Keep along the **L** edge of next field and cross stile. Next stile leads into Furzedown Wood.
❷ Descend through woodland (wonderful bluebells in spring), and into Wrinkle Wood, to meet lane.
❸ Turn **L**; there is limited parking for beach. Walk down Wonwell Slipway to look at Erme estuary, an attractive spot.
❹ Retrace your steps and follow coast path signs up steps **R** signed 'Bigbury-on-Sea'. Follow narrow wooded path, which leads along back of Wonwell Beach. Follow path along estuary to Muxham Point (with views to Meadowsfoot Beach).
❺ Path runs eastwards over stile (National Trust Scobbiscombe Farm), then sweeps across broad grassy area above Fernycombe Beach on to The Beacon, with views to Burgh Island ahead. Walk on through small gate above Beacon Beach. Follow undulating path through another gate. Path drops into steep combe before climbing (via gate) to reach bench on Hoist Point.
❻ Follow steep and difficult (often slippery) descent to quiet Westcombe Beach. Take care here.
❼ Turn **L** over stile at the back of beach, following signs for Kingston. Path has wire fence, **L**, and stream, **R**; cross wooden footbridge, **R**, over stream and enter willow plantation. Path twists on through strip of woodland.
❽ Cross over stile and straight on up pleasant, gradually ascending green lane (signed 'bridleway to Kingston'). Continue on to pass ponds at Okenbury, **R** (track is muddy in places). Track runs into tarmac lane, and back uphill into Kingston. At lane end turn **R**, then **L** to church and your car.

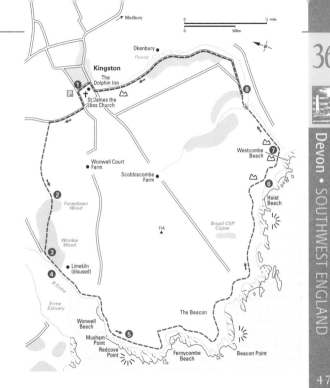

BIGBURY-ON-SEA Burgh Island Paradise
An art deco dream and Devon's oldest inn.

4 miles/6.4km 1hr 45min **Ascent** 246ft/75m ⚠ **Difficulty** 2
Paths Fields, tracks (muddy in winter) and coast path, 3 stiles
Map OS Explorer OL20 South Devon **Grid ref** SX 652442 **Parking** Huge car park at Bigbury-on-Sea

1 Leave car park through entrance. Follow coast path signs **R** (low tide route along beach to seasonal ferry to Bantham), then **L** towards road and **R** on to cliffs. Turn **L** before bungalows, then **L** to road. Cross, go through kissing gate and turn **R** uphill, passing through 2 big gates, to path junction near Mount Folly Farm.

2 Turn **L** along track (signed 'Ringmore'). At field top is path junction; go through kissing gate and keep ahead downhill, signed 'Ringmore', with fence **R**. Pass through metal gate, drop through kissing gate, keep ahead to another on farm track; walk up next field, crossing stile on to lane.

3 Cross over, following signs for Ringmore, through metal gate. Walk down into next combe, keeping hedgebank **R**. Cross stream at bottom on concrete walkway, and over stile. Ignore path **L**, but go straight ahead, uphill, through plantation and gate on to narrow path between fence and hedge.

4 Pass through kissing gate, bear **R** then turn immediately **L** uphill to path junction; pass through kissing gate and follow path to Ringmore. Turn **R** at lane, then **L** at church. Journey's End Inn on **R**.

5 From pub turn **R** down narrow lane which gives way to footpath. It winds round gardens to meet tarmac lane. Turn **L** downhill. Walk straight on down track, eventually passing Lower Manor Farm, and keep going down past 'National Trust Ayrmer Cove' notice. After small gate and stream crossing keep straight on at path junction.

6 Pass through kissing gate and walk towards cove on grassy path above combe (**L**). Pass through gates and over stile to gain beach.

7 Follow coast path signs ('Challaborough') **L** over small footbridge then climb very steeply uphill to cliff top and great views over Burgh Island. Cliffs are unstable here – take care. Path leads to Challaborough – huge holiday park.

8 Turn **R** along beach road and pick up track uphill along coast towards Bigbury-on-Sea. Go straight on to tarmac road, then bear **R** on coast path to car park.

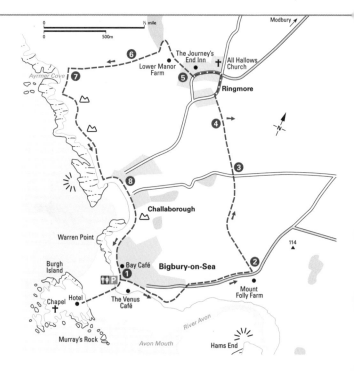

CADOVER BRIDGE Mysteries Of The Dewerstone

Industrial archaeology and a hard climb past the eerie Dewerstone Crags.

3.75 miles/6km 2hrs **Ascent** 180ft/55m ⚠ **Difficulty** 2

Paths Woodland paths, some rocky, 3 stiles
Map OS Explorer OL28 Dartmoor **Grid ref** SX 554645
Parking Free car park at Cadover Bridge

❶ Walk away from Cadover Bridge, with river on **R**. Pass through kissing gate and through small plantation. River is below to **R** with picnic spots along bank.

❷ Wooden ladder down bank leads to stile and footbridge into North Wood. Keep ahead on rocky path which follows course of large clay pipe, which appears above ground intermittently.

❸ Leave North Wood over stile. Follow path through open brackeny area; Plym is below on **R**. Path leads into silver birch and oak past settling tank, then forks. Take **R** fork downhill to path junction and gate.

❹ Turn **R** inside wire fence, following footpath sign 'Shaugh Bridge'. Stay within woods as yellow-waymarked path twists downhill. Path leads over stile to pass settling tanks (**R**), and eventually meets road.

❺ Turn immediately **R** and follow narrow path on and eventually down steps leading into Shaugh Bridge car park. Turn **R** through car park towards river.

❻ Cross river via railed wooden footbridge to enter Goodameavy (National Trust); look **L** to see

Shaugh Bridge and confluence of Plym and Meavy rivers. Follow path **R**. It becomes a restored track leading above river and winds steeply uphill. After sharp **L** bend take next path **R** (narrower but still paved). Continue uphill until level with top of granite buttresses (part of Dewerstone Crags) on **R**.

❼ Bear **R** and scramble steeply uphill, passing more buttresses (**R**). Eventually leave woods and enter open moorland to reach Dewerstone Rock.

❽ Turn 90 degrees **R** at rock and follow the **R-H** grassy path along edge of valley to pass Oxen Tor and over Wigford Down, keeping Cadworthy Wood and Plym Valley on your **R**. Keep straight on to boundary wall of wood, then follow wall around fields. Eventually wall bears **R** and you walk downhill past Cadover Cross with views of china clay works beyond. Bear **L** at cross to head towards bridge, cross over on road and return to car.

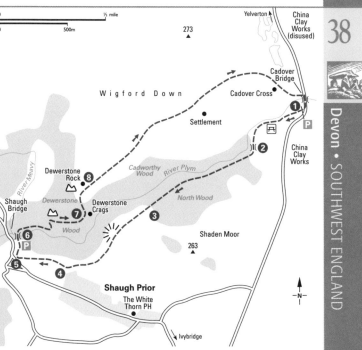

MELDON RESERVOIR Dartmoor's Highest Tors

An ancient oak woodland with views of Yes Tor and High Willhays.

4.5 miles/7.2km 2hrs **Ascent** 722ft/220m ⚠ **Difficulty** 2
Paths Grassy tracks and open moorland, some boggy patches **Map** OS Outdoor Leisure 28 Dartmoor
Grid ref SX 562918 **Parking** Car park at Meldon Reservoir (voluntary contributions)

❶ Walk up stone steps by toilets, through gate and go **L** on tarmac way towards dam, signposted 'Bridleway to Moor'. Cross over dam.

❷ Turn **R** along stony track. Soon gate (**R**) leads to waterside picnic area. Don't go over stile, but leave track here to go straight on, following edge of reservoir through side valley and over small footbridge. Narrow path undulates to steepish descent at end of reservoir to meet broad marshy valley of West Okement River; Corn Ridge, 1,762ft (537m), lies ahead.

❸ Pass small wooden footbridge and take narrow path along **L** edge of valley, keeping to bottom of steep slope that rises on your **L**. Path broadens uphill and becomes grassy as it rounds Vellake Corner above tumbling river below to **R**.

❹ At top of hill track levels and Blackator Copse can be glimpsed ahead. Follow river upstream past waterfall and weir, go **L** of granite enclosure, and along **L** bank through open moorland to enter Blackator Copse – wonderful picnic spot.

❺ Retrace your steps out of trees and bear **R** around copse edge, uphill aiming for **L** outcrop of Black Tor on ridge above. Pick your way through bracken to gain **L** edge of **L** outcrop. The **R** outcrop rises to 1,647ft (502m).

❻ Climb to top of tor if you wish; if not keep ahead in same direction, away from Blackator Copse, aiming for fairly obvious track visible ahead over Longstone Hill. To find it go slightly downhill from tor to cross 2 small streams, then pass between granite blocks marking track.

❼ Intermittent track runs straight across open moor. Where Red-a-Ven Brook Valley appears below to **R**, enjoy view of (**L** to **R**) Row Tor, West Mill Tor and Yes Tor. High Willhays, Dartmoor's highest point, lies just out of sight to **R**. Track bears **L** around end of hill, with good views towards quarry and viaduct, and drops back to reservoir.

❽ Bear **R** on track, then **L** over dam and back to car park.

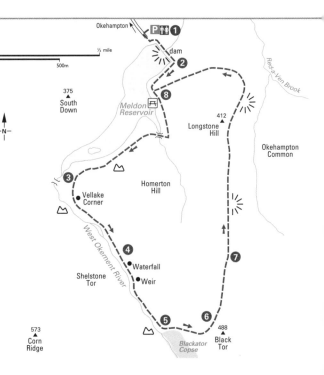

CLOVELLY Without The Crowds

Pheasants and follies – and a different way into Clovelly.

5.25 miles/8.4k 2hrs 15min **Ascent** 410ft/125m ⚠ **Difficulty** 2️⃣
Paths Grassy coast path, woodland and farm tracks, 4 stiles
Map OS Explorer 126 Clovelly & Hartland **Grid ref** SS 282260
Parking National Trust car park at Brownsham

❶ Follow footpath from back of car park, signed 'Buckland Woods'. Pass through gate into woods. Follow signs 'Footpath to coast path' to pass bench at path junction. Go straight on to cross stile and on to meet coast path.

❷ Go **R** over a stile (signed 'Mouthmill') into field on Brownsham Cliff. Good views ahead to Morte Point. Keep to **L** edge, across stile, down steps and **L** round field. Cross stile and zig-zag down through woodland. Leave trees; turn **L** towards sea at Mouthmill.

❸ Follow coast path across rocky beach. Clamber up rocky gully to meet track on bend; walk uphill (**L**).

❹ Eventually follow coast path signs **L**, then immediately **R**. Go **L** up wooden steps to follow narrow, wooded path uphill towards open cliff top at Gallantry Bower, with 400ft (122m) drop into sea. Re-enter woodland and follow signed path to pass 'Angel's Wings' folly. Where path leads straight on to church, keep **L** following signs and later via gate through edge of Clovelly Court estate. Enter laurel woods via kissing gate. Path winds past stone shelter, then through kissing gate into field. Keep to **L**; through gate and oak trees to meet road at big gate. Follow coast path signs on to road to top of Clovelly below Visitor Centre.

❺ Leave coast path and walk up deep, steep, ancient Wrinkleberry Lane (**R** of Hobby Drive ahead) to lane, past school and on to meet road. Turn **R**.

❻ Where road bends **R** go through gates to Clovelly Court. By church (**R**) follow bridleway signs **L** ('Court Farm & sawmills') through farm. At end of buildings keep ahead on track between fields. Pass through plantation, then bear **R** downhill across field as signed.

❼ Go through gate (by bridlepath sign). At bottom of field go through a gate into plantation, downhill.

❽ Turn **L** at forest track, following bridleway signs. Turn **R** as signed to cross stream and up long, gradually ascending track to Lower Brownsham Farm. Turn **L** for car park.

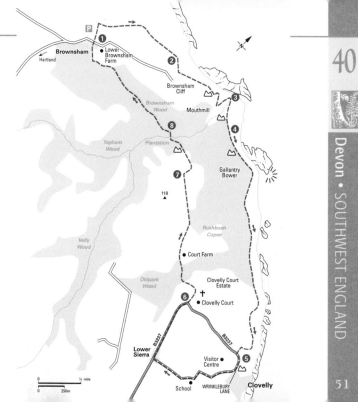

WIMBLEBALL LAKE Woodland Water

Through wooded valley, heath and across the mighty Wimbleball Dam.

Distance 6 miles/9.7km 3hrs **Ascent** 750ft/230m ⚠ **Difficulty** ③
Paths Rough descent, long climb, easy track between, 2 stiles
Map OS Explorer OL 9 Exmoor **Grid ref** SS 969285
Parking Frogwell Lodge car park, Haddon Hill

❶ Leave car park by kissing gate, which overlooks reservoir. Earth path down ahead crosses another earth track, and descends towards reservoir to meet tarred track. (**L** down this track leads to dam, Point ❸.) Cross and turn **R**, on rough track contouring to R. After 350yds (320m) this enters scattered birches. Turn down **L**, on smaller path, to meet stony track just above reservoir.

❷ Turn **L** on this to emerge into open grassland and start rising to **L**. Watch out for stile down on R, into woodland. Across this, turn **L** on small path to emerge near Wimbleball Dam. Side-trip on to dam gives fine views of Hartford Bottom below.

❸ Return along dam and turn **R** into descending tarmac track signed 'Bury 2.5'. At bottom keep ahead on path signed 'Bridleway'. With a bridge ahead, bear **L** on to grass track, signposted 'Bridleway to Bury'. It leads to ford, look for footbridge on **R**. Once across, take track between houses, to turn **L** out into Hartford.

❹ Turn **L** ('Bury 2') on well-used track. Pass through woods beside River Haddeo. Track becomes tarmac as it enters Bury.

❺ Turn **L** to packhorse bridge beside road's ford. Ignore riverside track on **L** and continue for 180yds (165m) to turn **L** at bridleway sign, 'Haddon Hill'. Here pass between houses and ahead into sunken track. This climbs steeply, stream at bottom. At top it continues as green (or brown) track between grown-out hedges, before turning **L** for Haddon Farm.

❻ Pass to **L** of farmhouse, on its access track. After 0.25 mile (400m) reach corner of wood. As track is concreted on steep section, look for stile above leading into wood. Go up the **L-H** side of wood to gate on to open hill at top corner.

❼ Take track that bears **L** to cross crest of hill. With views ahead to Brompton Regis, turn sharp **R** on wide track to top of Haddon Hill. Continue downhill, on wide track through open moor to car park.

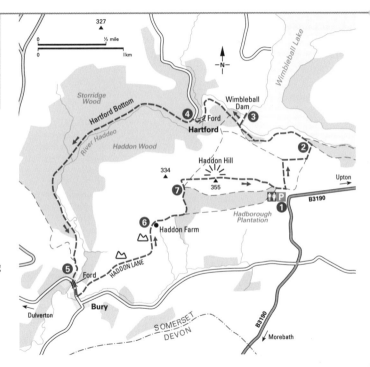

HORNER Exmoor's Red Deer

On the trail of Exmoor's red deer in the woodlands under Dunkery Beacon.

4.5 miles/7.2km 2hrs 30min **Ascent** 1,000ft/305m ⚠ **Difficulty** ③
Paths Broad paths, with some stonier ones, steep in places, no stiles
Map OS Explorer OL 9 Exmoor **Grid ref** SS 898455
Parking National Trust car park (free) at Horner

❶ Leave car park in Horner past toilets and turn **R** to track into Horner Wood. Cross bridge and pass field before rejoining Horner Water. You can take footpath alongside stream instead of track, they lead to same place. Ignore 1st footbridge; continue along obvious track to where sign, 'Dunkery Beacon', points **L** towards 2nd footbridge.

❷ Ignore this footbridge as well. Keep on track for another 100yds (91m), then fork **L** on path alongside West Water. This rejoins track, and after another 0.5mile (800m) alongside track is another footbridge.

❸ Cross to path that slants up **R**. After 200yds (183m) turn **L** into smaller path that turns uphill alongside Prickslade Combe. Path reaches combe's little stream at cross-path, with wood top visible above. Here turn **L**, across stream, on path contouring through top of wood. After dip and climb, emerge into the open and arrive at view over top of woodlands to Porlock Bay. Join bridleway near lone pine with bench.

❹ Continue ahead on grassy bridleway, with car park of Webber's Post visible ahead. In 55yds (50m), fork down **L** on clear path back into birchwoods. This zig-zags down to meet larger track in valley bottom.

❺ Turn downstream, crossing footbridge over East Water, beside ford. After 60yds (55m) bear **R** on to ascending path. At top of steep section turn **R** on sunken path up **R** to Webber's Post car park.

❻ Walk to **L**, round car park, to Horner. (Or take the pink-surfaced, easy-access path immediately to **R**.) Path runs immediately below 'easy access' one with its stone bench. Just after concrete sculpture where easy access turns back, bear **L** on wider path, soon passing wooden hut. Fork **L** on wider path to keep ahead down wide, gentle spur, with valley of Horner Water **L**. As spur steepens, footpath meets crossing track signposted 'Windsor Path'.

❼ Turn **R** for 30 paces, then take descending path signposted 'Horner'. Narrow at first, this widens and finally meets wide, horse-mangled track with wooden steps; turn **L** down this into Horner.

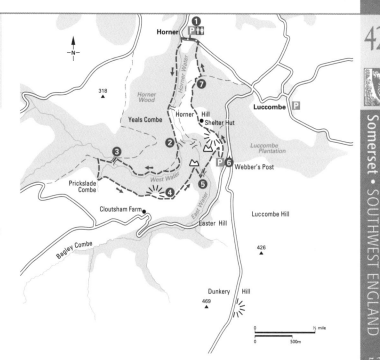

LYPE HILL To Brendon's Heights

From Wheddon Cross up to the high point of the Brendons.

5.75 miles/9.2km 3hrs **Ascent** 850ft/260m ⚠ **Difficulty** 3
Paths A rugged track, then little-used field bridleways, 2 stiles
Map OS Explorer OL 9 Exmoor **Grid ref** SS 923387
Parking Village car park (free) on A396 at Wheddon Cross

❶ From main crossroads head towards Dunster, and bear **R** at war memorial to pass small car park on **R-H** side. After school, bear **R** following signpost to Puriton (Popery Lane). Sunken lane runs to Cutcombe Cross; keep ahead ('Luxburough via Putham Ford') then bear **L** at sign into Putham Lane.

❷ Horses and tractors also use narrow hedged track. At bottom it crosses ford, with stone footbridge alongside. Keep ahead on to climbing lane surfaced with eroded tarmac.

❸ At top of steep climb field gate on **R** has footpath signpost, 'Lype Hill'. It leads on to green track that runs below and then into wood. Gate on **R** leads to less-used track. In 100yds (91m) turn down **R** across stream, with yellow spots and posts marking small path uphill to its **R**, into open space. Slightly wider path above slants up along bracken clearing. After gate it follows foot of wood, to join forest road and then reach tarred lane.

❹ Turn **L**, down wide verge, and take upper of 2 gates on **R** with stile and footpath sign. Head up, beech bank **L**, to cross top of wooded combe. Stile and gate ahead. Don't cross, but turn **R**, and **R** again across top of field to gate beside trig point on Lype Hill.

❺ Through gate keep ahead across field, with tumulus 70yds (64m) on **L**, and after gate bear **L** to follow fence on **L** to its corner. Gate ahead leads on to road. Cross to signposted gate, and bear **L** to field's far corner. Turn **L** alongside beech bank to waymarked gate. Don't go through gate, but turn **R** along fence to smaller gate. Continue downhill with fences on your **R** and then hedge on your **L**, towards white-walled Pit Leigh Farm. Gate leads to driveway just to **L** of farm.

❻ Cross driveway into green track. This becomes fenced-in field edge to gate on **L**. Turn **R** to continue as before with hedges now R. After 2 fields reach hedged track. This runs down to crossroads in Popery Lane and to return to Wheddon Cross and car park.

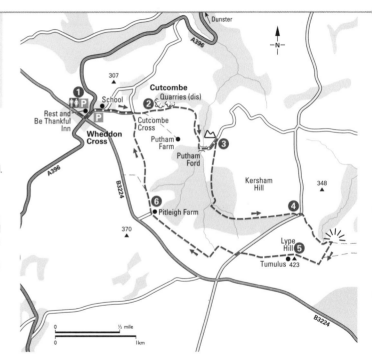

KILVE Along The Quantock Coastline

A stimulating walk including Tudor villages, breezy cliffs and industrial remnants and geology underfoot.

3 miles/4.8km 1hr 30min **Ascent** 250ft/76m ⚠ **Difficulty** ☐1
Paths Tracks, field paths, and grassy cliff top, 4 stiles **Map** OS Explorer 140 Quantock Hills & Bridgwater
Grid ref ST 144442 **Parking** Pay-and-display at sea end of Sea Lane

❶ From car park head back along lane to ruined chantry. Turn into churchyard through lychgate. Pass to **L** of the church, to reach kissing gate.

❷ A signposted track crosses field to gate; bear **R** to another gate and pass along foot of East Wood. (At far end, stile allows access into wood, April to August only.) Ignoring stile on **L**, keep ahead to field gate with stile and track crossing stream.

❸ Track bends **L** past gardens and ponds of East Quantoxhead to tarred lane. Turn **R**, towards Tudor Court House, but before its gateway bear **L** into car park. Pass through to tarred path and kissing gate. In open field this bears **R**, to St Mary's Church.

❹ Return to kissing gate, don't go through, instead bear **R** to field gate, and cross field beyond to distant gate and lane. Turn **R** and, where lane bends L, keep ahead into green track. At its top, turn **R** at 'Permissive path' noticeboard.

❺ Follow field edges, with hedges on your **R**, down to cliff top, and turn **R**. Clifftop path leads to kissing

gate before sharp dip, with ruined lime kiln opposite. This was built around 1770 to process limestone, which was shipped from Wales, into lime for the fields and for mortar. Foreshore below the kiln is limestone, but it was still easier to bring it by sea across Bristol Channel.

❻ Turn around head of dip, and back **L** to cliff top. Here iron ladder descends to foreshore: you can see alternating layers of blue-grey lias (a type of limestone) and grey shale. Fossils can be found here, but cliffs are unstable – hard hats are now standard wear for geologists. Continue along the wide clifftop path until tarred path bears off to **R**, crossing stream studied by Coleridge. As you come into car park, on your **L** is the brick chimney of a short-lived Oil Retort House (for oil distillation) from 1924; there is oil in grey shale, but it's probably less trouble to get it from Texas.

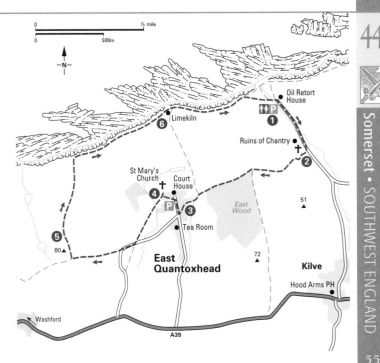

45

Somerset • SOUTHWEST ENGLAND

HOLFORD A Quantock Amble

An up-and-down walk in the glorious Quantock combes.

5.5 miles/8.8km 2hrs 40min **Ascent** 1000ft/305m **⚠ Difficulty** 2
Paths Wide, smooth paths, with one slightly rough descent, no stiles **Map** OS Explorer 140 Quantock Hills & Bridgwater **Grid ref** ST 154410 **Parking** At back of Holford (free)

❶ Two tracks leave road beside car park. Take the **R-H** one, marked with bridleway sign. It becomes earth track through woods, with Hodder's Combe Brook on its **R**. After 0.75 mile (1.2km) small track fords stream and forks. Take R-H option, entering side valley. Path runs up valley floor, crossing to **R-H** side of stream – ignore further side valley and path forking **L**. Go up gently through oakwoods floored with bilberry (locally known as 'whortleberry'), then mixed heather and bracken, to reach Quantock ridge. As ground eases, keep ahead over 2 cross-tracks to Bicknoller Post.
❷ Just behind oak post turn **R** then keep slightly **L** and uphill on widest of tracks. This track becomes double one, almost 'dual carriageway'. Bear **L** off it to trig point on Beacon Hill.
❸ At trig point bend half **R** to another marker post on 'dual carriageway' track. Smaller path goes down directly ahead, into Smith's Combe. Path weaves around, crossing stream several times.

❹ At foot of valley, with green fields below, is a 4-way 'Quantock Greenway' signpost: turn **R** ('Holford'), uphill at first. Path runs around base of hills, with belt of trees below and then green fields. At 1st spur crest is another signpost: keep ahead for Holford. Path runs around base of hills, with belt of trees below and then green fields. It drops to cross a stream, Dens Combe. After 0.25 mile (400m) reach junction with wide gate leading out on tarmac.
❺ Don't go through gate, but strike uphill to another 'Quantock Greenway' signpost. Keep **L** to pass above pink house on to tarred lane. Follow it ahead below couple of houses. Lane runs out past Alfoxton, with walled garden of grand house (once Wordsworth's, now hotel) on **L** and stable block with its clock on **R**. At foot of hotel driveway is small parking area.
❻ Follow lane for 650yds (594m) then, as it bends **R**, look out for waymarker and railings down in trees. Below is footbridge leading across into Holford. Turn **R**, and at 1st junction turn **R** again, to car park.

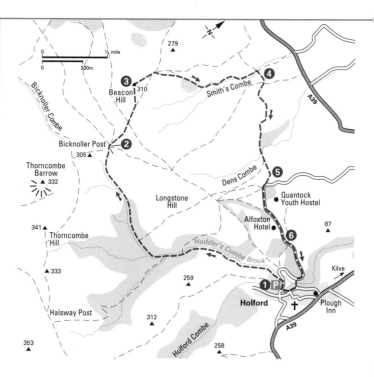

WIVELISCOMBE Wool Town And The Tone

A pretty village and a wooded riverside on the edge of the Brendons.

6 miles/9.7km 3hrs 15min **Ascent** 1,000ft/300m ⚠ **Difficulty** 1
Paths Tracks, a quiet lane, a few field edges, 2 stiles
Map OS Explorer 128 Taunton & Blackdown Hills **Grid ref** ST 080279
Parking North Street, Wiveliscombe

❶ Turn **L** out of car park into Square, head down High Street and turn **L** at traffic-lights into Church Street. Turn **R**, down steps under arch, to Rotton Row. Continue to South Street and turn **L** along pavement past school.

❷ At end of village (house No 2) turn **R**, along lane, and go ahead through gate with footpath sign. Cross stile ahead, and bottom edges of 3 fields. Stile in hedge ahead has grown over, so head up **L** for 30yds (27m) to gateway before returning to field foot to pass through farm buildings. Continue ahead up **L-H** edge of field above to gate leading on to B3227.

❸ Turn **L**, then **R** into lane downhill. After 0.75 mile (1.2km) it crosses River Tone and bends **L** at Marshes Farm. Keep ahead, on track marked by bridleway sign. Do not turn **R** here on track towards Wadham's Farm, but keep uphill to join upper farm track. Turn **R** to top of deeply sunken lane. Turn **R** in this, descending towards farm, but at 1st first buildings turn **L**. This track runs up River Tone. With houses ahead, turn **R** to cross footbridge and turn **L** to Challick Lane.

❹ Track continues upstream beside River Tone through pleasant woodland to reach Washbattle Bridge.

❺ Turn **R**, up road, for 200yds (183m). Forest track, with footpath signpost, leads uphill on **R**. With pheasant fence alongside, bear **L** on to wide path that continues uphill. At wood edge, exit through field gate and then turn **R**, to cross bottom corner of field to more woodland opposite. Turn uphill alongside this to gate beside concrete water tank.

❻ Go through gate and turn **L**, with hedge on **L**. Next gate opens on to hedged track. This turns R, and passes reservoir at summit of Maundown Hill. At top of tarred public road turn sharply **R** on to track that becomes descending, hedged path. At signposted fork turn **L** on to contouring path. Soon tarred lane leads down into town, with car park near by on **L**.

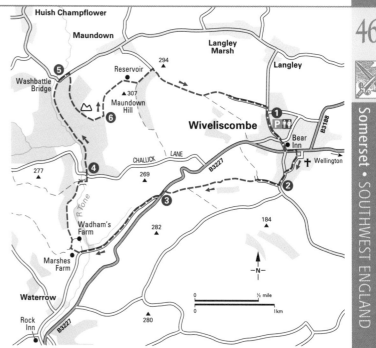

47
STAPLEY Close To The Border
Stapley's little valley looks down over the county boundary into Devon.

3 miles/4.8km 1hr 40min **Ascent** 500ft/152m ⚠ **Difficulty** ①
Paths Field edges, and small woodland paths, 14 stiles
Map OS Explorer 128 Taunton & Blackdown Hills **Grid ref** ST 188136
Parking Small pull-in beside water treatment works at east end of Stapley; verge parking at walk start

❶ Phone box marks start. Some 20 paces below, lane runs between houses. After 100yds (91m) keep ahead into shady path. At stile bear **R** to ford with footbridge. ❷ Head up wide track. At junction cross on to small, waymarked path that's muddy to start with. This heads uphill, following bank, to stile. In field beyond (nettles in season) bear **R**, to field corner and stile back into woodland. Small path runs along top edge of Paye Plantation, to emerge near Beerhill Farm. ❸ Bear **L** for 100yds (91m) to waymarked gate below farm, and 2nd just beyond. Keep ahead, below farm and above wood, to gate with cattle trough. In field beyond, follow top edge of wood to Rainbow Lane. ❹ Cross lane to signposted stile. Pass along **L** edge of long narrow field. After this field, stile leads into ash trees. Again path runs along top edge of wood. With isolated house visible ahead, waymarker indicates diverted right of way bearing **R**. This path slants gently downhill, to meet house's driveway at bend. Cross to

wide path above driveway. At end of wood turn down **R**, to rejoin driveway to road below. ❺ Cross into trackway of Biscombe Farm. Bear **L** to field gate, and go down **R** edge of large field to stile in hedge gap on **R**. Slant down following field to stile at its bottom, **R-H** corner, with stepping stones across stream beyond. Go up **R-H** edge of next field to stile. This leads into sunken track; turn **L** and follow it up to lane. (If track is impossibly soggy, turn **L** along field top and through gate to join it higher up.) ❻ Turn **R** to walk up road. Where road levels and bends **L**, turn **R** into driveway of Craigend Cottage to find stile where driveway bends **R**. Turn **L** along field tops, with hedge bank on your **L** and view of Devon over **R** shoulder. At end of 2nd field, gate leads to tractor track. After short, muddy passage past Stapley Farm you reach village road at phone box.

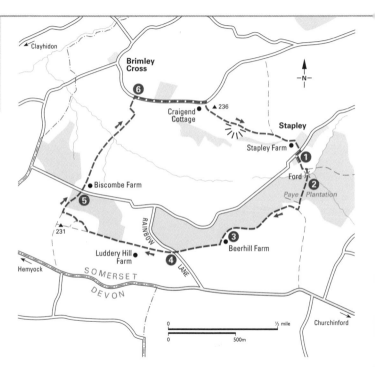

BLACKDOWN HILLS Prior's Park Woodlands

Prior's Park Wood is at its best with autumn's colours or spring's bluebells beautifully concealing some intricate geology.

5 miles/8km 2hrs 40min **Ascent** 700ft/213m ⚠ **Difficulty** 2
Paths Rugged in Prior's Park Wood, otherwise comfortable, 7 stiles
Map OS Explorer 128 Taunton & Blackdown Hills **Grid ref** ST 211182
Parking Roadside pull-off between post office and Blagdon Inn

❶ Walk starts at phone box opposite Blagdon Inn. Cross stile and follow **L** edge of triangular field to another stile into Curdleigh Lane. Cross into ascending Quarry Lane. Pass between buildings of Quarry House, on to track running ahead up into and through Prior's Park Wood.
❷ From mid-April this wood is delightful with wild garlic and foxtail grass (actually sedge). Track is also fine (but possibly muddy) in autumn. Keep uphill, ignoring side-path **L**. Main path eventually declines into muddy trod, slanting up and leftwards to small gate at top of wood.
❸ Pass along wood's top edge to gate. Cross next field between fences to Prior's Park Farm, passing between its buildings to its access track and road. Turn **L** and follow road with care, as it's fairly fast section, towards Holman Clavel Inn.
❹ Just before inn turn **L** on to forest track. Where track ends small path runs ahead, zig-zagging down

before crossing stream. At wood's edge turn **R** to walk up wider path to reach B3170.
❺ At once turn **L** on lane signed 'Feltham'. After 0.5 mile (800m) wide gateway on **L** leads to earth track. This runs along top of Adcombe Wood for 0.5 mile (800m), then down inside it. Once below wood follow track downhill for 180yds (165m). Look for gate with signpost on **L-H** side and go through it.
❻ Follow hedge on **R** to a stile and footbridge, then bend **L**, below foot of wood, to another stile. Ignore stile into wood on **L**, but continue along wood's foot to next field corner. Here further stile enters wood but turn **R**, beside hedge, to tarmac track. Turn **L**, then bear **R** along Curdleigh Lane, back into Blagdon Hill.

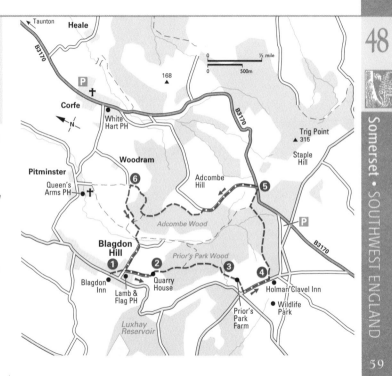

Somerset · SOUTHWEST ENGLAND

59

ILMINSTER A Walk In The Woods

A pleasing riverside and woodland ramble.

5.75 miles/9.2km 2hrs 40min **Ascent** 500ft/152m ⚠ **Difficulty** 1

Paths Tracks, wide paths, and riverside field edges, 4 stiles
Map OS Explorer 128 Taunton & Blackdown Hills **Grid ref** ST 361146
Parking Wharfe Lane pay-and-display, off Canal Way; or West Street; or by Donyatt Church, Point ⑤

❶ From Market Square head uphill on North Street. With Bell Inn on **L**, route continues on path (Old Road). It rises past beacon fire-basket and mobile phone mast before descending to B3168.
❷ Cross carefully into hedged byway to Eames Mill. Turn **R**, along waymarked track. After 220yds (201m) concrete track turns sharply back **L**. Before bridge, go through chain gate to follow River Isle upstream.
❸ Cross weir to head upstream, river **L**. After 1 mile (1.6km), and ignoring 2 bridges over river, reach Powrmatic works car park, and chain gate to B3168.
❹ Cross B3168 and then follow track signed 'Rose Mills Industrial Estate'. Pass along river bank to **L** of buildings, then between piles of ironwork and round to **R** of large white shed to footbridge. With river on your **R**, head upstream in fenced way to re-cross on another footbridge. Continue crossing stiles along **R-H** bank. With tower of Donyatt church ahead, cross diagonally **R** to gate by thatched cottage on to road.

❺ Turn **L** through village, and bear **L** past church. Head up Herne Hill as lane leads to track, then field edge path, then earth path through Herne Hill Wood. Summit is under tall beeches. Wide avenue ahead leads to field corner. Continue just inside wood, passing bench and trig point on **R**, and descending to wood's foot. Keep **R**, to corner of wood, before path bends back **L** alongside field fence to gate on **R**.
❻ Wide path runs towards Ilminster, with sports fields below. Turn **L**, between sports fields and town, for 200yds (183m) to yellow litter bin and green shed. Gap on **R** leads to path alongside murky remnant of Chard-Taunton Canal. Turn **R** behind tennis courts, and after 250yds (229m) turn **L** into Abbots Close and on to tarred path. This leads to West Street, arriving at Crown Inn. Turn **R** and bear **R** into Silver Street, to reach town centre and car park.

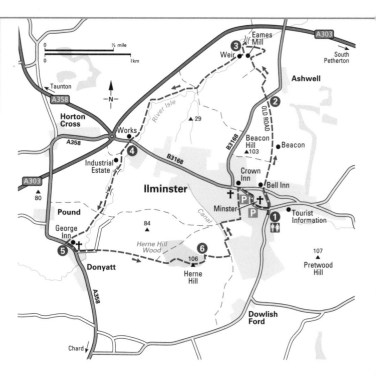

HAM HILL Golden Stone

Ascending the hill of warm-coloured limestone.

4 miles/6.4km 2hrs **Ascent** 700ft/213m ⚠ **Difficulty** 2

Paths Well-trodden and sometimes muddy, 2 stiles
Map OS Explorer 129 Yeovil & Sherborne **Grid ref** ST 478167
Parking View Point car park on western escarpment of Ham Hill

❶ Turn **R** out of car park (big, westward view on R) to road junction. Keep **L** for 35yds (32m) then take path on **R**, signed 'Norton Sub Hamdon'. This leads through woods around side of Ham Hill, keeping at same level, around rim and then just below it, all way round. When open field appears ahead, path turns R, downhill.

❷ Ignore 1st gate on **L** but go down through 2nd. Descend grassland into small valley with hummocks of medieval village of Witcombe. Head **L** up valley floor, passing to **L** of willow clump. Grassy path slants up **R-H** side of valley to field corner. Here turn **L** on track leading to lane near Batemoor Barn.

❸ Hollow Lane descends directly opposite. Gate and gap just to **R** lets you pass along field edges, then into wood. Just inside wood, turn **R** up steps. Clear path runs just below top of wood, then down to edge of Montacute village. Turn **L** to pass entrance to Montacute House, to reach King's Arms pub.

❹ Turn **L**, past church; after duck pond turn **R** on permissive path. Kissing gate leads to base of St Michael's Hill. Turn **L** for 150yds (137m) to stile into woods.

❺ Path ahead is arduous. For gentler way up hill, turn **L** around its base to gateway and stile at foot of descending track. Otherwise cross stile to very steep path, to summit tower. Tower is open and spiral staircase is well worth climb. Descend winding main track to gateway and stile at hill's foot.

❻ Turn half **R** and go straight down field to gate at its bottom corner. This leads on to track corner. Turn **L** and follow track round field corner. After 90yds (82m) take **R** fork. Earth track runs close to foot of woods, passing ruins of pump house, and diminishing to path; it then climbs steps to join higher one. Turn **R** to continue close to foot of woods until path emerges at gate after 500yds (457m). Steps lead up to Prince of Wales pub. Turn **L** along its lane, through hummocks of former quarries, to car park.

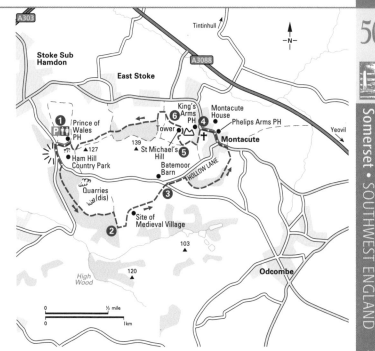

CUCKLINGTON Deepest Somerset

Up hill and down, taking in a church with over a thousand years of history.

5.5 miles/8.8km 2hrs 45min **Ascent** 600ft/183m ⚠ **Difficulty** 3

Paths Little-used field paths, which may be overgrown, 11 stiles
Map OS Explorer 129 Yeovil & Sherborne **Grid ref** ST 747298
Parking Lay-by on former main road immediately south of A303

❶ With A303 on **R**, walk along lane to where track runs ahead into wood. At far side fenced footpath runs near main road. Turn **L** up path, then **R** into fenced-in path and bear **L** to Parkhouse Farm. After nettly passage (summer) to **L** of buildings, turn **L** to lane.
❷ Turn back **R**, to follow field edge back alongside farm track. Go through field gate and at once turn **L** through another. Aiming towards Stoke Trister church, follow **L** edge of field and then go straight up 2nd, turning **R** along lane to church.
❸ Continue for 170yds (155m) to stile and gate on **L**. Go up track, but turn **R** alongside hedge above, passing mobile phone mast on **R**. Follow hedge around rim of Coneygore Hill, over stile, to 2nd.
❹ Head down towards Stileway Farm. Half-way down, turn **L** and contour across fields to stile, and then to gate with cattle trough and stile above. (Or track just above farm leads across into this same field's foot.) Head uphill, with hedge now on **L**, to steeper

bank around Coneygore Hill. Turn **R** and follow this banking to cross stile. Keep level through tree gap, then slant down to **R**, below vineyard, to stile behind. Path ahead contours forward to lane near Manor Farm.
❺ Turn downhill past thatched cottage, and bear **R** for Cucklington. There are field paths on **L**, but it's simpler to use this lane to cross valley and climb to Cucklington village. Gravel track on **L** leads to Cucklington church.
❻ Pass to **L** of the church, and contour across 2 fields, passing above Cucklington Wood. In 3rd field slant up to **R** to track, which leads to Clapton Farm.
❼ After Tudor manor house track bends **R**, uphill. Turn **L** between farm buildings to gate beside phone mast, then turn **L** again down wooded bank. Turn **R**, along base of bank, to gap in grown-out hedge. Bear **L** past power pole to field's bottom corner. Cross footbridge under hazels to 2nd and stile beyond. Go straight up to stile by cattle trough and lane and car.

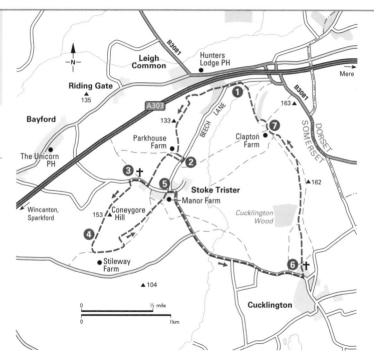

SOUTH CADBURY Cadbury Castle As Camelot?

Cadbury castle hill-fort gives wide views of Somerset and a glimpse of pre-history.

6.5 miles/10.4km 3hrs 30min **Ascent** 1,000ft/305m ⚠ **Difficulty** ☐2

Paths Well-used paths, 7 stiles

Map OS Explorer 129 Yeovil & Sherborne **Grid ref** ST 632253

Parking Cadbury Castle car park (free), south of South Cadbury

❶ Turn **R** out of car park to 1st house in South Cadbury. Stony track leads up on to Cadbury Castle. Earth ramparts and top of fort are Access Land, so stroll around at will.

❷ Return past car park. After 0.25 mile (400m) pass side road on L, to stile marked 'Sigwells'. Go descend to stile and footbridge. Follow **L** edge of field then uncultivated strip. Track runs ahead, but take stile on **R** to follow field edge next to it, then line of hawthorns ahead, to gate with 2 waymarkers. Faint track leads along top of following field. At end turn down into hedged earth track. This leads past Whitcombe Farm to rejoin road.

❸ Turn **L** to junction below Corton Denham Beacon. Keep **R** for 80yds (73m) to stile up L. Backtrack above hedge to steep spur of Corton Hill, and go up it (or more gently slant up **L** above trees), to summit trig point.

❹ Head along steep hill rim with steep drops to Corton Denham on **R** and soon with fence on L. Pass

small, covered reservoir. Above, 5 large lime trees slant gently down to small, waymarked gate. Green path slants down again, to gate to tarred lane; follow this until to road below.

❺ Turn **L** on road, which is narrow between high banks, for 170yds (155m) to stile on **R**, 'Middle Ridge Lane'. Go straight across, **L** of tree and ditch line, to hidden stile into lane. Keep ahead on stony track that climbs gently to ridgeline.

❻ Turn R, and walk along Corton Ridge with hedge on **R** and wide view on L. After 650yds (594m) Ridge Lane starts on **R**, but go through small gate on **L** to continue along ridge. After final gate, green path bends around flank of Parrock Hill. With Cadbury Castle now on **L**, main path turns **L** to hedge corner and waymarked gate. Hedged path leads to road.

❼ Cross into road signed 'South Cadbury'. After 700yds (640m) turn **R**, again for South Cadbury, and follow road round base of Cadbury Castle to car park.

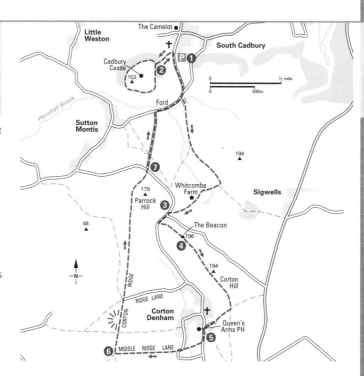

POLDEN HILLS Edge Of The Levels

From Polden's edge down on to the Somerset Levels and up again.

4.5 miles/7.2km 2hrs 15min **Ascent** 450ft/137m **⚠ Difficulty** 2

Paths Initially steep then easy tracks and paths, 3 stiles

Map OS Explorer 141 Cheddar Gorge **Grid ref** ST 480345

Parking Car park (free) at Street Youth Hostel, just off B3151; another car park on south side of road

1 From parking area on youth hostel side, cross and turn **R** on woodland path. After 100yds (91m) smaller path descends on **L** by some steps. At foot of wood turn **R**, and at field corner go down to reach track. This runs along base of wood to lane.

2 Go down to entrance of Lower Ivy Thorn Farm, and turn **L** into track. After 0.5 mile (800m) this reaches corner of unsurfaced road, where you turn **R**. After 0.25 mile (400m) track turns **L** into field. Follow its edge, with ditch and fence to **L**, to gate at field corner. In next field continue alongside ditch to corner. Former footbridge is derelict under brambles. Take gate on **L**, then turn **R**. Field edge zig-zags to pass to **L** of Hurst Farm, leading to tarred lane.

3 Turn **R** to reach bridleway sign on **L**. Follow green track until it joins Ham Lane. Follow lane to reach crossroads of B3151 in Compton Dundon, with Castlebrook Inn to your **R**.

4 Cross busy B3151 and pass between market cross

(**R**) and granite Victorian obelisk (**L**) into Compton Street. At 1st junction keep round to **L**, towards Hood Monument above. As street starts to climb, turn **R** and **L** up lane beyond, signposted 'Butleigh'. Where it reaches woodland bear **R**, up steep fenced path, ignoring stiles on **L**. Path slants up into wood. Then, some 35yds (32m) before it arrives at road, turn **L** along top of steep ground, to Hood Monument.

5 Continue down through wood to minor road, with main road 50yds (46m) away on **R**. Ignore path descending opposite but turn **R** for few steps to footpath sign and kissing gate. Grass path heads gently up crest of Collard Hill, with wide views to **L**.

6 From summit go straight on down to stile and signposted crossroads of B3151. Cross both roads. Ridge road is signposted for youth hostel, your path is just to its **R**. Cross glade into woodland. Keep to **R** of some hummocky ground to wood's edge, and follow path to car park.

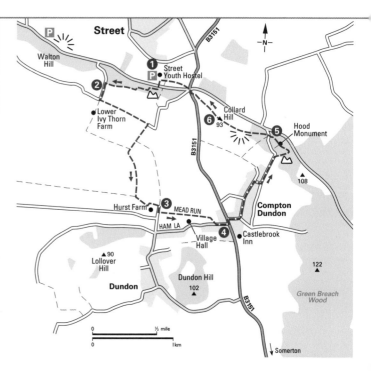

BRUTON Golden Wool

A walk around and above a typical Somerset wool town.

4.5 miles/7.2km 2hrs 15min **Ascent** 350ft/107m ⚠ **Difficulty** 2

Paths Enclosed tracks, open fields; no stiles
Map OS Explorer 142 Shepton Mallet **Grid ref** ST 684348
Parking Free parking off Silver Street, 50yds (46m) west of church; larger car park in Upper Backway

❶ With church on **L** and bridge on **R**, head down Silver Street to car park in Coombe Street. Old bridge over River Brue leads into Lower Backway. Turn **L** for 350yds (320m); take path between railed fences to footbridge. Turn **R** along river to A359.
❷ Turn **R** over Leggs Bridge and **R** again into end of High Street, but at once turn uphill on to walled path 'Mill Dam'. At lane above turn briefly **R**, then **L** along byway track signed 'Creech Hill Lane'. After footbridge fork **L**: hedged path is steep and muddy. At top of combe it becomes farm track. This bends **L** (short-cut track on **R** isn't right of way) and reaches Wyke Road.
❸ Turn **R** few steps, then **R** again, and after 220yds (201m) turn **R** past farm buildings to track, Creech Hill Lane. This becomes hedged tunnel then emerges at Creech Hill Farm. Past hedge hiding slurry pit is fine view over Bruton. Pass front of farm and out to B3081.
❹ Head up road to 1st field gate opposite, with bridleway signpost. Turn sharp **R** to pass below hedge. Small path follows rim of combe hollow. Opposite

Green's Combe Farm, slant down **L** to below stream junction – strips of trees mark streams. Cross stream and bear **L** to gate on to farm's driveway track.
❺ Turn **R**, away from farm, for 220yds (200m) until track bends **R**. Keep ahead through field gate with blue waymarker, on to green track. After 200yds (183m), at foot of former hedge, turn downhill, to **L** of row of hazels, to gate. Pass through wood to gate and track. Emerge into open field, follow fence above to join B3081. Turn **L**, uphill, to entrance to Coombe Farm.
❻ Ignoring stile on **L**, go down driveway dozen paces before turning and at once forking **L** again on to wide path under sycamore trees. Path rises gently, with bank on its **L**. At clearing, keep to **L** edge to find descending path that becomes St Catherine's Hill. Weavers' cottages are on **R** as street descends steeply into Bruton. Turn **L** along High Street. At end turn **R** down Patwell Street to Church Bridge.

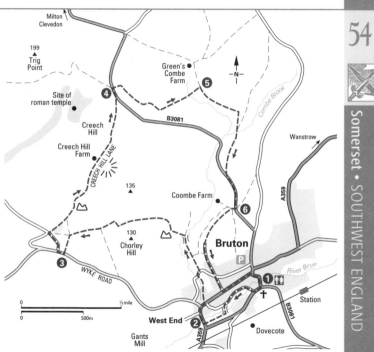

NUNNEY Castle And Combe

Through woodland and pasture, visiting a stone-built village with a moated castle.

3 miles/4.8km 1hr 15min **Ascent** 160ft/49m ⚠ **Difficulty** 1

Paths Broad, riverside path, pasture, then leafy track, no stiles

Map OS Explorer 142 Shepton Mallet **Grid ref** ST 736456 **Parking** Short-stay parking at Nunney Market Square; small lay-by at end of a public footpath 150yds (137m) up Castle Hill

❶ From Nunney's Market Place cross brook and at once turn **R** to Nunney Castle (entry is free). Having inspected castle, cross footbridge towards church. Turn **L** in Church Street, past stone cross. In another 55yds (50m), where street starts uphill, go **L** into Donkey Lane.

❷ Follow lane past high wall on **L**, to gate with signpost. Keep ahead, leaving track after 150yds (137m) for small gate ahead into woods. Wide path leads downstream with Nunney Brook on its **L**. After about 0.75 mile (1.2km) track runs across valley.

❸ Turn **L**, as signpost suggests, to cross brook; immediately turn **R** past broken stile. Continue along stream on often muddy path. After 350yds (320m) path climbs away from stream to join track above. Turn **R** on this, to cross stream on high, arched bridge. Track bends **R**, through gate: as it bends back round to **L** keep ahead to waymarked kissing gate on **L**.

❹ Go up **R-H** side of narrow field to kissing gate.

Continue uphill on **L-H** edge for 65yds (60m) to kissing gate in hedge. Turn up **R**, next to hedge, then **L** along top of field to gap at its corner. This is crest of broad ridge with views ahead to hills in east.

❺ Head down **L-H** side of field into slight dip. Ignore half-hidden stile on **L** but go through gateway ahead. Now turn half-**R** and go straight across field to visible kissing gate in skyline hedge – this turns out to be 2 gates, 1 behind the other. Once through these, follow **L-H** edge of long field ahead. At its corner take kissing gate between 2 gateways and turn **R**. Same direction as before, but now with hedge on your **R**. At field end cross farm track via 2 gates. In another 150yds (137m), kissing gate is on your **R**.

❻ This leads into narrow track between over-arching hedges. It bends to **L** and then **R**, then descends to become street leading into Nunney. This runs down to join Donkey Lane on outward route, with church 300yds (274m) ahead.

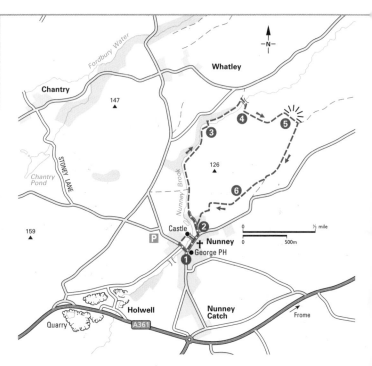

BURROW MUMP On The Levels

A gentle wander around the Somerset Levels near Burrowbridge leading up to a hump called a 'mump'.

5.25 miles/8.4km 2hrs 15min **Ascent** 150ft/46m ⚠ **Difficulty** ②
Paths Tracks, paths, unfrequented field edges, 2 stiles
Map OS Explorer 140 Quantock Hills & Bridgwater **Grid ref** ST 360305
Parking Grid reference: Parking: National Trust car park (free) at Burrow Mump

❶ Gate leads on to base of Mump. Circle hill's base to **L** to small gate and steps down to Burrow Bridge. Just before bridge turn **R** into Riverside. After 350yds (320m) turn **R** into Burrow Drove, which becomes tractor track. On either side and between fields are deep ditches, coated in green pondweed. At T-junction there's culvert of 19th-century brick on **L**. Here turn **R** on new track round **L** of Burrow Wall Farm, to A361.
❷ 'Public footpath' sign points to track opposite. After 30yds (27m) turn **L** over stile. With bushy Burrow Wall on your **R**, cross field to usually muddy Grove Farm. Go through 2 gates below wooded bank rising to continue along fields, to **R** of buildings, on **L**. At corner of 2nd field awkward rusty gate leads up between brambles to green track: turn **R** here to reach lane near Pathe (farm).
❸ Turn **R** along lane, ignoring track on **R**, to reach side-lane on **R**. Here cross bridge to hedge-gap on **R** and very narrow footbridge. Continue through several fields, with wide ditch on **R**. Near by, on **L**, is low

banking of Challis Wall, concealing the Sowy River. Ditch on **R** gradually gets smaller. When it finally ends bear **R** to River Parrett and follow it to latticework road bridge. Cross this into Stathe.
❹ Keep ahead through village past Ludwells Farm, to reach kissing gate on **R** waymarked 'Macmillan Way'. Follow **R** edge of field to gatepost; cross to hedge opposite and follow it round to **L**, to stile. Continue ahead with hedge on your **R**, to where hedged track leads to road. Turn **L**, scrambling up banking, to walk on Southlake Wall between road and river.
❺ As road turns away from river, rejoin it. Once across Stanmoor Bridge you can bear **R** (if not too nettly) for river bank path to Burrowbridge. Turn **R** across bridge and, this time, climb to top of Burrow Mump for fine views of Somerset.

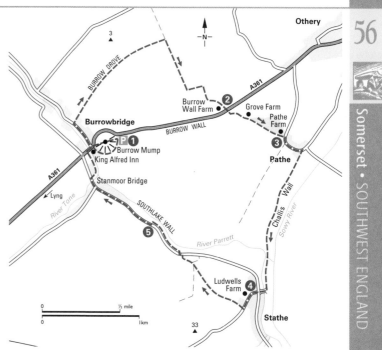

EBBOR GORGE Coleridge's Inspiration

The small but sublime limestone gorge that inspired the poet Samuel Taylor Coleridge.

4.75 miles/7.7km 2hrs 30min **Ascent** 1000ft/305m ▲ **Difficulty** ③
Paths Small paths and field edges, with a rugged descent, 10 stiles
Map OS Explorer 141 Cheddar Gorge **Grid ref** ST 521484
Parking Lane above Wookey Hole or Wookey Hole's car park below Point ❷

❶ From noticeboard at top end of car park descend stepped path. After clearing, turn **L**, signposted 'The Gorge'. Wide path crosses stream to junction.
❷ Turn **R**, away from gorge down valley to road. Turn **L**, to pass through Wookey Hole village. At its end road bends **R**; take kissing gate on **L** with 'West Mendip Way' post. After 2 more kissing gates turn **L** up spur to stile and top of Arthur's Point.
❸ Bear **R** for 60yds (55m) into woods again. Path now bears **R** to stile. Go down **L** to kissing gate back into wood. At once, and before lime kiln just ahead, turn up **L** between boulders to pass between high quarry crags. Bear **R** along wood foot to join short track ahead. It leads to 4-track junction with waymarker post standing in stone plinth.
❹ Turn sharp **L**, on to tarred track that bends **R** then **L** through Model Farm, to Tynings Lane. Turn **L** for 85yds (78m) to signposted stile on **R**. Go up with fence on your **R**; bear **L** to gate with stile. Go straight

up next field, aiming for gateway below top **L** corner with tractor ruts running into it. Track leads up through wood and field. From gate at its top slant upwards in same direction to another gate next to stile 100yds (91m) below field's top **L** corner.
❺ Small path runs along tops of 3 fields with long view across Levels away to your **L**. With stile on **R** and gate and horse trough in front, turn downhill keeping fence on your **R**; follow it to stile leading into Ebbor Gorge Nature Reserve.
❻ 2nd stile leads into wood. At junction with red arrow and sign marked 'Car Park' pointing forward, turn **R** into valley and go down it – this narrows to exciting, rocky gully. At foot of gorge turn **R**, signposted 'Car Park'. You are now back at Point ❷ of outward walk. After crossing stream turn **L** at T-junction to wood edge, and back **R** to car park.

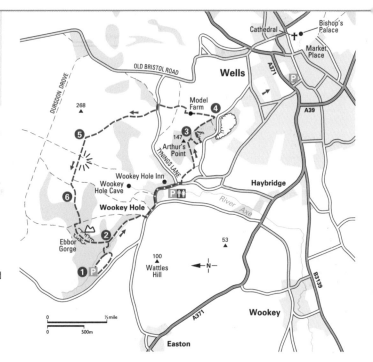

CROOK PEAK The Western Mendips

A high-level ridge wander in the western Mendips to Somerset's shapeliest summit.

6 miles/9.7km 3hrs **Ascent** 900ft/274m ⚠ **Difficulty** ☐2
Paths Field edges, then wide clear paths, 7 stiles **Map** OS Explorer 153 Weston-super-Mare
Grid ref ST 392550 **Parking** On road between Cross and Bleadon, west of Compton Bishop; also street parking in Cross and on A38

❶ Cross road to wide gate on **R** (not small gate ahead). Wide path contours round through brambly scrub, crosses ridge line and drops through wood and then along its foot to gate. Just below, lane leads down into Compton Bishop. Turn **L** to church.
❷ Lane turns down, before church, to crossroads. Take track opposite and follow it round bend to its end. You will now contour round base of high slope of Wavering Down. Cross stile, pass through wrought-iron gate into narrow paddock, and cross another stile into large field; keep along bottom edge of this. At its corner keep ahead over stile, then across foot of 3 more fields. Move 40yds (37m) uphill around fence corner to another stile on same level. Follow long bottom edge of field, then cross another under power line, to track and turn **R**, down to road. Turn **L** through Cross village.
❸ At 'Give Way 150yds' sign (warning of A38 ahead) turn **L** up steep rocky path. It turns **R** above fence, then slants up to rejoin same fence higher up. It enters

woodland, running just above foot of wood, through 2 gates. Now wide earth path, it finally emerges at top of car park located on Winscombe Hill.
❹ Turn **L**, away from car park, on broad track, uphill. This rises through King's Wood, then dips slightly to pass pantiled Hill Farm, before rising to trig point on Wavering Down. Continue with wall on your **R** to cross Barton Hill. In dip below Crook Peak wall ends. Waymarkers point to **L** and **R**, but keep ahead to climb slightly crag-topped summit.
❺ Turn **L** and (with small rocky drop down to your **L**) head down on to long gentle ridge – outcrops of limestone poke out through shallow grass. At railed barrier turn **R** on path back to car park.

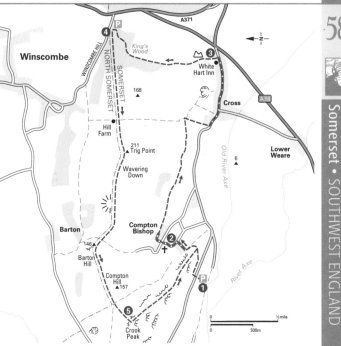

DOLEBURY WARREN An Iron Age Hill-Fort

A walk on the northern rim of the Mendips.

5.25 miles/8.4km 2hrs 30min **Ascent** 750ft/229m ⚠ **Difficulty** 1

Paths Wide and mostly mud-free, 4 stiles **Map** OS Explorer 141 Cheddar Gorge

Grid ref ST 444575 **Parking** Pull-off near church; street parking in Shipham centre

❶ From war memorial crossroads in centre of Shipham village head uphill on Hollow Road (signposted 'Rowberrow'). At top bear **R** into Barn Pool, and at end turn **R** into Lipiatt Lane. At lane's top end, keep straight ahead on path with waymarker for Cheddar, to descend sunken path to stream.

❷ Just before stream turn **L** on path marked 'Rowberrow'. Stay to **L** of stream (ignoring fork off to **R**) – path becomes track. After passing 3 houses and lime kiln, at start of tarmac, turn **R** into forest at noticeboard, 'Rowberrow Warren'.

❸ Track bends to **R**, climbing. At corner of open field turn **L** into smaller track that descends gently with this field above on its **R**. At junction keep ahead, uphill, for 35yds (32m) then turn **L** on forest track with bridleway sign.

❹ After 350yds (320m) bear **L** down gradually shrinking track, soon with young spruce above on **R**. Where it joins stony track below, bear **R** on stony track, with wall to your L. At T-junction turn **L** for 90yds

(82m) to gate on **L** with National Trust sign.

❺ Follow grassy ridgeline ahead, along line of thorn trees, then passing along **L** side of fenced enclosure of scrubland. Bear **R** ('Limestone Link' waymarker) to pass to **R** of tall pine clump. Emerge on to more open grassland with wide views. Highest point of ridge is rim of huge Dolebury hill-fort.

❻ Green track runs down through fort and into woods below. It bends **L**, then back **R**, to emerge at gate on to tarred lanes. Take lane on **R**, down to A38. Cross to signposted bridleway: this leafy path with bedrock bottom rises to lane. Turn up **L** – ground on **L** consists of broken stones from disused Churchill Quarry below. Ignore turnings to **L** and **R** and follow enclosed track down to Star.

❼ Cross A38 on to grass track to stile, and go up grassy spur above. Keep up next to some trees on your **R** to stile, and pass to **R** of football pitch, to find short path out to edge of Shipham. Turn **R**, to village centre.

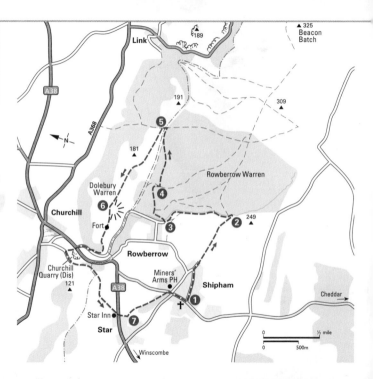

WOOLLARD Hunstrete And Compton Dando

Serenity in a rich landscape nestling between the cities of Bristol and Bath.

6.25 miles/10.1km 3hrs 30min **Ascent** 700ft/213m ⚠ **Difficulty** 2
Paths Tracks, field paths, woodland paths, and byways, 11 stiles
Map OS Explorer 155 Bristol & Bath **Grid ref** ST 632644
Parking Street parking near bridge in Woollard; also opposite pub in Compton Dando (Point ❻)

❶ From crossroads take road 'Hunstrete' across River Chew; bear **R** at 'Circular Walk' sign. Byway is underwater at first, but path parallels it on **R**. At high point, where byway becomes tarred, turn **L** through gate into Lord's Wood. Wide path descends, crossing track, to pool. Pass to **L** of this, to waymarker and track junction. Track opposite leads up to edge of wood.
❷ Turn **R**, and drop to hidden footbridge under trees. Head uphill, passing **R-H** edge of plantation, to Pete's Gate beside corner of Hunstrete Plantation. Turn **L** to field gate. Turn **R**, around field corner, to go through gate. Continue along same hedge, bending **R** at field end, to reach lane at edge of Hunstrete.
❸ Turn **L** beside Cottage No 5. Go down **R-H** side of field to stile into Common Wood. Track ahead passes through paintball area. After it crosses stream and bends **L**, take signposted path to top of wood. Pass through col with lone ash tree, and keep ahead, across field to short hedged path. Go straight down **L** edge of field to signpost; turn **R** to join lane at Marksbury Vale.

❹ Turn **L** towards Court Farm; just before buildings turn **R** over stile, and take **R-H** track for 100yds (91m) to stile on **L**. Pass to **R** of farm buildings to rough track following Bathford Brook. Head downstream to reach track at Tuckingmill.
❺ Follow track past manor house to ford. Cross footbridge and turn **R**, alongside stream, again line of underwater byway – rejoin it as it emerges. It leads to road, with Compton Dando 700yds (640m) away on **L**.
❻ Turn **R** into Church Lane, and then go through lychgate. Stile leads down steps. Turn **L** behind mill house and pass to **L** of mill pond, to footbridge.
❼ Bear **L** into Park Copse. At its top follow **R-H** edge of field round to stile. In lane beyond turn **L**; it becomes hedged track and runs past tiny gorge as it descends to Woollard.

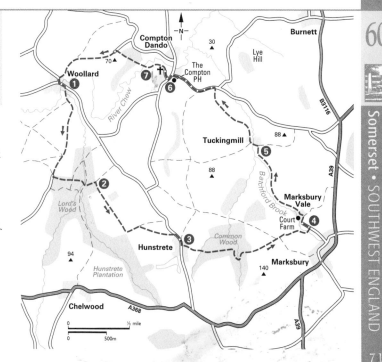

HENGISTBURY HEAD Heights And Huts

An easy coastal loop with much to see.

3.25 miles/5.3km 1hr 45min **Ascent** 109ft/33m ⚠ **Difficulty** 2

Paths Grass, tarmac road, soft sand, woodland track, some steps
Map OS Explorer OL22 New Forest **Grid ref** SZ 163912
Parking Car park (fee) at end of road, signed 'Hengistbury Head' from B3059

❶ From corner of car park take gravel path towards sea, with fenced-off lines of Double Dikes to your **L**. At sea-edge you can see for miles each way:.

❷ Turn **L** and follow road along cliffs. Priory Church in Christchurch dominates view inland across harbour, with St Catherine's Hill behind. Follow road up hill. Pause to admire boggy pond on your **R**, home to rare natterjack toad. Road narrows; climb up some steps, passing numbered post marking Stour Valley Way. As you climb steep path, views back along coast are fabulous, and there are views across shallows of Christchurch Harbour, usually buzzing with windsurfers and sailing dinghies.

❸ On heathy top of Warren Hill viewing platform tells you that you're 75 miles (120km) from Cherbourg and 105 miles (168km) from Jersey. Keep **R** along path, passing deserted coastguard station and following top of cliffs. Descend into deep hollow, where sea appears to be breaking through. Keep straight on, following

curve of head. At end, path turns down through some trees; descend steps. Walk along sparkling, white sand on sea side of beach huts to point. Stone groynes form little bays.

❹ At end of spit you're only stone's throw from opposite shore (ferry runs across to pub from end of pier, passed further on). Turn round end of point, passing old Black House, and walk up inner side of spit, overlooking harbour.

❺ If you've had enough beach, you can catch land train back to car park from here (times vary seasonally). Otherwise, join metalled road which curves round to **R** past freshwater marsh and lagoon.

❻ At post marked '19' turn **R** on to dirt path and follow it briefly through woods, crossing small ditch, to emerge back on road. Turn **R**, passing extensive reedbeds on **R** and bird sanctuary on **L**. Continue past thatched barn and follow road to café, ranger station building and car park.

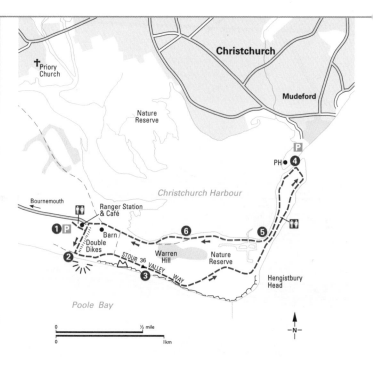

HORTON The Rebel King

A luscious landscape, where once a rebel was roused.

7.5 miles/12.1km 4hrs **Ascent** 426ft/130m ⚠ **Difficulty** 2

Paths Field paths, tracks, some road, 19 stiles
Map OS Explorer OL22 New Forest; Explorer 118 Shaftesbury & Cranborne Chase
Grid ref SU 034072 (on Explorer 118) **Parking** Lay-by with phone box, just west of Horton

❶ Go towards village, turn **L** over stile by pump. Head to Horton Tower, over 2 stiles. Go diagonally **L** uphill. Cross fence at top corner; turn **R** for tower.
❷ Retrace steps; stay on track through gate into Ferndown Forest. After 0.25 mile (400m) bear **L** on to firmer track. Shortly, turn **R** between trees. Cross stream and track to gate.
❸ Pass this, go through bank and turn **L** along forest ride. Turn **R** before edge of wood; follow path for 0.75 mile (1.2km). Bear **L** at bottom, down track. Turn **L** at crossroads; pass Paradise Farmhouse.
❹ Turn **L** between houses; follow road to Holt Lodge Farm. With buildings **L**, bear half-**R** across yard to grassy lane.
❺ Continue to end of field, with hedge to your **R**. Cross stile and turn immediately **L** through gate to Early's Farm. Then bear **R**, in front of house, into lane. At junction after Chapel Farm, turn **L** ('Long House'), turn **R** at next one and cross stile. Bear **L** around field, cross stile behind house and stile to road.

❻ Turn **L**, then **R** into lane by Pee Wee Lodge. Keep ahead at junction; fork **R** into Grixey Farm. Follow waymarker uphill, crossing 2 stiles. With copse on **L**, go up field. Cross stile and turn **L** on to road.
❼ After 0.5 mile (800m) bear **L** ('Monmouth's Ash Farm'); take path to **R** of bungalow. Keep straight on bridleway over heath and into woodland. After 1 mile (1.6km) metalled road emerges from woods.
❽ At Woodlands Manor Farm walk to **R** of golf club gates and turn **L** over stile along road with fence. Bear down to **R** beside lake and stay on road. After it becomes track, look for 2 stiles in hedge on **R**, just after farm. Cross these and go diagonally across field to 2 more stiles. Bear **R** to corner of next field and another 2 stiles, turning **R** to meet road.
❾ Turn **L** through Haythorne but, before road descends, go **R**, through trees, to gate and down field, to emerge by vineyard. Turn **L** and **L** again to car.

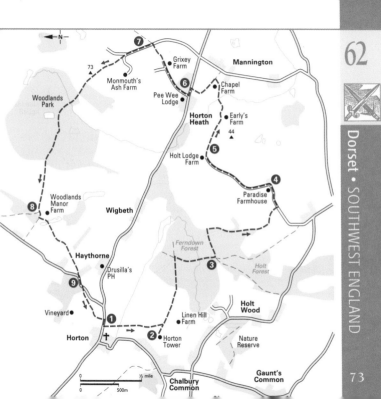

STUDLAND Sand And Heath

Easy walking through a nature reserve over beach and heath.

Distance 7 miles/11.3km 3hrs 30min **Ascent** 132ft/40m ⚠ **Difficulty** 1
Paths Sandy beach, muddy heathland tracks, verges
Map OS Explorer OL15 Purbeck & South Dorset **Grid ref** SZ 033835
Parking Knoll car park (fee), by visitor centre, just off B3351

❶ From car park go past visitor centre to sea. Turn **L** and walk up beach for about 2 miles (3.2km). Marram-covered dunes hide edge of heath on your **L**, but you have views to Tennyson Down on Isle of Wight, and golden cliffs of Bournemouth curve away ahead. Continue round tip of sand bar into Shell Bay. Poole opens out ahead – more precisely, spit of Sandbanks, with white Haven Hotel facing you across harbour mouth. There are good views of nature reserve Brownsea Island.

❷ Turn inland at South Haven Point, joining road by phone box. Pass boatyard and toll booth, then bear **R** at gate on to bridleway leading down to some houseboats. Turn **L** along the inner shore of Poole Harbour and past Bramble Bush Bay. Choose any of tracks up to road. Cross and then follow verge until end of some woods on your **L**, when you can pick up broad muddy track on heath. After 0.5 mile (800m) this bends **L**. Where track bends sharply **R** to meet

road, stay ahead on footpath for another 220yds (200m).

❸ Cross road by bus stop and head down track, indicated by fingerpost. Go past marshy end of Studland Heath and up to junction by Greenlands Farm. Bear **L** and, just round next corner, turn **L** through gate on to heath. Go straight along old hedge-line, pass barn on **L**, and reach fingerpost.

❹ Turn **L** across heath (not shown on fingerpost), aiming for distant lump of Agglestone. Go through gate by another fingerpost and continue along muddy track over top, passing Agglestone away to your **R**. Go down into some woods, turn **R** over footbridge and pass through gate into lane. Pass several houses then, where blue markers indicate public bridleway, turn **L** into field. Head diagonally **R** into green lane and go through gate at bottom. Turn **L** along verge, pass Knoll House Hotel and turn **R** at signpost to return to car park.

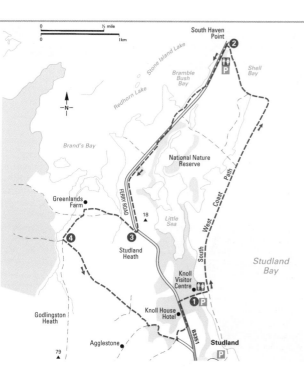

SWANAGE The Extraordinary Collector

A coastal town that not only exported stone but imported it too.

4.25 miles/6.8km 2hrs 30min **Ascent** 509ft/155m **⚠ Difficulty** ☐2
Paths Grassy paths, rocky tracks, pavements, 4 stiles
Map Explorer OL15 Purbeck & South Dorset **Grid ref** SZ 031773
Parking Durlston Country Park (fee)

❶ Take footpath directly below visitor centre car park, signed to Tilly Whim and coast path. Steps lead down through some trees. With sea ahead, follow path round to R, joining coastal path. Keep R, towards lighthouse, down steep path. As you climb up other side, look back and down to admire spectacular Tilly Whim Caves cut into ledges of cliff. Pass lighthouse and turn R, then go through kissing gate to follow path with butterfly markers up steep side of Round Down.
❷ At top bear R, heading inland and parallel with wall. Go down slope, through gate and across footbridge, then turn up to R. At wooden gate turn **L** over stone stile, following butterfly marker. After another stile you can see Purbeck Hills ahead. Cross stile and go down track. Beyond stile by farm track narrows and starts climbing. Continue straight ahead on to road and follow this into town, with prominent church in front.
❸ Turn **R** on to main road. Continue along street, but

look out for modest metal plaque above front door of No 82A, home of Taffy Evans who died with Captain Scott on return from South Pole; elaborate Wesley memorial; and Town Hall with its Wren frontage.
❹ At square bear **L** beside Heritage Centre, towards harbour. Turn **R** and pass entrance to pier. Follow fingerpost to coastal path, then bear R, up hill, past modern apartment block and stone tower, to reach tip of Peveril Point, with coastguard station.
❺ Turn **R** and walk up grassy slope along top of cliffs. Take path in top corner and follow Victoria's head markers to road. Turn **L** through area of pleasant Victorian villas. Erosion of coastal path means well-signed detour here, along street, down to **L** and **L** through gate into woodland, signposted to visitor centre and lighthouse. Follow path for about 0.5 mile (800m) along cliff top to Durlston Head. Pass Durlston Castle on your **L** and turn down to examine Burt's great stone globe. Climb back up steep hill to car.

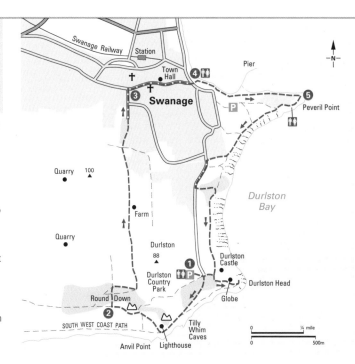

64

Dorset • SOUTHWEST ENGLAND

75

CRANBORNE CHASE The Royal Forest

Extensive plantations on the landscape of a Norman royal hunting forest provide superb walking.

4 miles/6.4km 2hrs **Ascent** 165ft/50m ⚠ **Difficulty** 2

Paths Woodland paths and tracks, quiet roads, farm paths, 3 stiles

Map OS Explorer 118 Shaftesbury & Cranborne Chase **Grid ref** SU 003194

Parking Garston Wood car park (free), on Bowerchalke road

1 Go through gate in corner and take broad track that leads up through woods. Go straight ahead through kissing gate and emerge at corner of field. Keep **R**, up edge of this field, and continue straight on. **2** At junction of tracks turn **L** and walk alongside hedge, on waymarked bridleway, through farmland dotted with trees. Muddy farm track leads downhill. Where it sweeps **L** into farm, go straight ahead on grassy track. Pass cow byres on **L**, with Upwood farmhouse largely hidden in some trees ahead, and turn **R** along lane. Continue through gate, along old avenue of sycamores between high banks and hedges. **3** Pass house on **R** and bear **L** on steep, narrow path straight down hill to emerge on road, in hamlet of Deanland. Turn **R**, pass phone box and reach gate on **L**, with yellow marker. Go through, bear diagonally **R** across small field to cross stile, then bear **L** up edge of field, with woods to your **L**. **4** Look for stile on your **L**, but turn directly **R** here, to

walk across field, parallel with road. Over brow of hill ahead, higgledy-piggledy settlement of New Town can be seen. Head for stile in bottom corner of field. Turn **L** up lane, which becomes woodland track. Follow this for 0.5 mile (800m). By entrance to conifer wood, named Great Forlorn, look for yellow marker and turn **R** uphill. After climb it levels out, with fields on **L**. Keep straight on, with good views across to West Chase house, at head of its own valley. Descend steadily, then cross stile to emerge at road by lodge house. **5** Cross straight over on to broad track and immediately turn up to **R** on narrow path beside fence. Follow this straight up hill through woods – it levels out towards top, with fields on **L**. At junction of tracks keep **L** then bear **R**, continuing along edge of wood, and eventually descending to reach road. Turn **R** to return to car park.

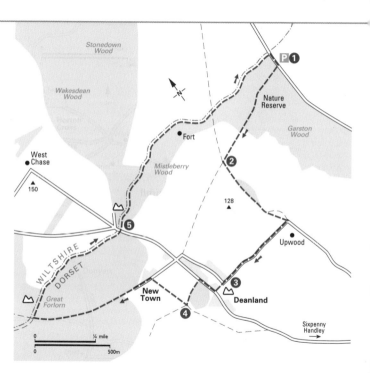

BADBURY RINGS Roads And Residents

An easy, longish walk on the edge of the Kingston Lacey Estate.

7.5 miles/12.1km 3hrs 30min **Ascent** 459ft/140m ⚠ **Difficulty** 2

Paths Farm tracks, roads, grassy lanes and fields, 14 stiles
Map OS Explorer 118 Shaftesbury & Cranborne Chase **Grid ref** ST 959031
Parking Car park (donation) at Badbury Rings, signposted off B3082 from Wimborne to Blandford

❶ Walk up hill to explore site of Badbury Rings, then head down track by which you drove in. Cross B3082 and go down road towards Shapwick. Pass Crab Farm on your R, with Charborough Tower on horizon.

❷ At junction with Park Lane turn **R**, then **R** again by Elm Tree Cottage to go up Swan Lane, grassy track. Turn **L** over stile before gate. Go straight over field, cross stile, and along next field edge. Cross stile into Bishops Court Dairy yard and turn **R** past 1st barn. At gates bear **L** over stile, then **R** across field, heading for stile half-way along hedge. Cross this and bear **R** to top corner of field.

❸ Cross stile and turn **L** down broad bridleway. After about 0.5 mile (800m) pass line of trees. Turn **R**, up track between high hedges (following blue public bridleway marker). Continue walking downhill, with glimpses of Tarrant Crawford church blending into trees on **L**. Follow track round to **L**, by side of stream.

❹ Go through gate and reach church on **L**. Continue towards barns of Tarrant Abbey Farm. Go **L** through

gate and continue diagonally across field to track between fences. Follow this uphill, passing above farmhouse. At top of track cross stile and go straight over next field. Cross road and walk down edge of field. Go over stile and cross road into green lane. Bear **L** across stile and diagonally across field. Go through gate on to road and turn **R**.

❺ Walk on to old Crawford Bridge, to admire it. Retrace steps and turn **R** at footpath sign. Cross stile and walk straight across meadows for 1 mile (1.6km). When you reach fence on **L**, walk around it to gate. Go through and follow track round to **R**. Cross stile behind farm and walk along road into village.

❻ Pass Anchor pub and turn **L**, passing Piccadilly Lane on your **R-H** side. Go straight up road, retracing route back to car park at Badbury Rings.

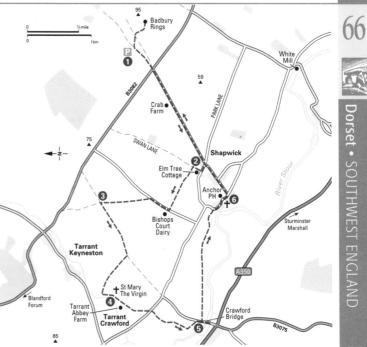

Dorset • SOUTHWEST ENGLAND

ASHMORE Roaming The Woods

A gentle amble through plantations of mixed woodland to a village highpoint.

5.75 miles/9.2km 2hrs 30min **Ascent** 427ft/130m **⚠ Difficulty** 1

Paths Forestry and farm tracks, woodland and field paths **Map** OS Explorer 118 Shaftesbury & Cranborne Chase **Grid ref** ST 897167 **Parking** At Washers Pit entrance to Ashmore Wood

1 With back to road, walk past barrier and follow firm forestry road as it curves past beeches of Washers Pit Coppice **L** and Balfour's Wood **R**. After 0.5 mile (800m) ignore crossing bridleway and stay ahead on track. You're now in Stubhampton Bottom, following winding valley through trees.

2 Where main track swings up **L**, keep ahead, following blue public bridleway marker, on rutted track along valley floor. Path from Stony Bottom feeds in from **L** – keep straight on. Where exposed hillside appears on **L**, follow blue markers on to narrower track to **R**, which runs down through coppiced woodland parallel and below forestry road. At Hanging Coppice marker post shows where Wessex Ridgeway path feeds in from **R** – again, keep straight ahead. Path soon rises to emerge at field corner.

3 Turn **L** at fence (follow blue marker), walk uphill. Follow path along edge of forest with lovely views to southeast.

4 After 0.75 mile (1.2km) turn **L** at track junction (signposted 'Ashmore') and walk through woods. Cross track and keep straight on, following blue marker, to meet track. Go straight on, following signs for Ashmore, soon emerging from the forest; ignore 2 **L** turns. Continue straight up track for 1 mile (1.6km), through farmland and across exposed open hilltop, with houses of Ashmore appearing. At end of track turn **R** and walk into village to pond.

5 Retrace route but stay on road out of village, passing Manor Farm on **R** and heading downhill. Just before road narrows to single track width, bear **L** through gate (blue marker). Walk along top of field, pass gate on **L** and bear down to **R** to go through lower of 2 gates at far side. Walk straight ahead on broad green track. Go through gate into woods and immediately turn **R**, following steep bridleway down hillside to emerge by car park.

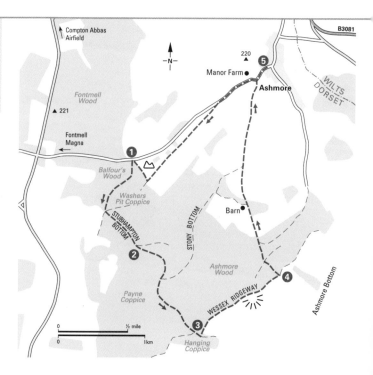

COMPTON ABBAS Wild Flowers And Butterflies

Over the preserved downs around Compton Abbas, in search of butterflies and wild flowers.

4.5 miles/7.2km 2hrs **Ascent** 820ft/250m ⚠ **Difficulty** 2

Paths Downland tracks, muddy bridleway, village lanes, 1 stile

Map OS Explorer 118 Shaftesbury & Cranborne Chase **Grid ref** ST 886187

Parking Car park on road south of Shaftesbury, with NT sign for Fontmell Down in bottom **L** corner

❶ Take rough track from bottom **R** corner of car park, walking downhill towards Compton Abbas. Pass old chalk quarry. Soon turn **R** up wooden steps and cross stile to Compton Down. Bear **L** and uphill towards fence, and eventually join it at corner. Carry on to **R** alongside fence, heading towards saddle between down and Melbury Hill.

❷ Pass steep, natural amphitheatre on **L**, head diagonally **L** to fingerpost and gate at saddle, and turn **L** on either side of fence. Follow this to top of Melbury Hill – steep climb but good views. Pass scar of ancient cross dyke, on **L**, and look down other side to silvery tower of Melbury Abbas church.

❸ Toposcope marks hill top, with fantastic views all around, including Shaftesbury on ridge north and ridges of Hambledon Hill southeast. Retrace route to signpost and gate and turn **R** across grass, joining track coming in from **L**. Shortly, at end of field below, bear down steeply **L** to 3 gates and go through 2 of them. Head straight along field edge towards Compton

Abbas. Pass through gate onto road.

❹ Turn **L** and follow road **R** round sharp bend. Pass tower of original church, in small graveyard. Continue along lane, passing houses. Descend between high hedges and turn **L** at junction. Continue on winding road through bottom of village, passing thatched cottages, with spire of modern church ahead trees.

❺ Pass Clock House and turn **L** up bridleway, signposted 'Gore Clump'. Gravel track gives way to tree-lined path between fields. Go through gate and straight on. Go up **R** edge of this and next field. In corner, turn **L** along fence and walk up track above trees to gate and NT sign for Fontmell Down. Pass through this on to Fontmell Down. Continue ahead on rising track. After 0.5 mile (800m) ignore stile to **R** and keep ahead along fence, to top of hill and car park.

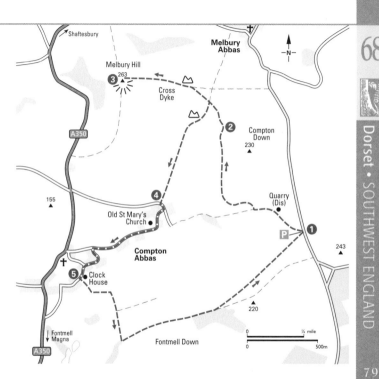

HAMBLEDON HILL A Famous Landmark

Take the gentle route of a famous sculpted landmark.

4.5 miles/7.2km 3hrs **Ascent** 541ft/165m ⚠ **Difficulty** 1

Paths Village, green and muddy lanes, bridleways, hillside, 5 stiles

Map OS Explorer 118 Shaftesbury & Cranborne Chase **Grid ref** ST 860124

Parking Lay-by opposite Church of St Mary's

❶ With church on **L**, walk up street. Pass farmhouse on corner of Main Street and Frog Lane. Turn **R** and follow Frog Lane out of village. Just after crossing River Iwerne, go **L** through kissing gate, on path alongside field edge near river.

❷ Cross footbridge and continue to **R** along river. Reach track by Oyle's Mill and turn **L** along it. After 0.5 mile (800m), pass Park Farm, on R, and keep ahead. At junction bear **R** into Bessells Lane.

❸ At end, by The Lynes, bear **R** and immediately **L** up muddy bridleway, with trees **L**. Keep forward at junction where trees end, and at top bear **L** down narrow lane, part of defensive ditch at foot of hill. At road turn **L** and head into Child Okeford. Just past postbox turn **L** and cross stile. Bear **R** along park edge, towards church tower. When you get to fence turn **L**.

❹ Cross drive and keep straight on, glimpsing chimneys of Victorian manor house to **L**. At end cross stile and bear **L** down path. Cross stone stile by road

and immediately turn **L** up lane. This becomes track, climbing steeply through trees.

❺ Bear **R** in front of nature reserve sign and follow track uphill. Path levels below earthworks ringing hilltop. Emerge from track and bear diagonally **L** up open grass to top.

❻ At trig point turn **L** to explore ancient settlement. Return to trig point, turn **L** over top of hill and descend slope, following bridleway.

❼ Meet track by wall at bottom. Turn **L** and go through gate, with village ahead. Follow track down to cricket pavilion. Through gate turn **R**, on to road. Follow this past thatched barn and turn **R** to return to car.

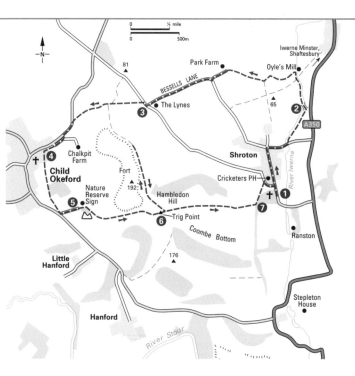

FIDDLEFORD Ancient Mills And A Manor House

Two ancient mills and an extraordinary manor house, along the banks of the River Stour.

5.25 miles/8.4km 3hrs **Ascent** 429ft/150m ⚠ **Difficulty** 2
Paths Grassy paths, muddy woodland tracks, a rutted lane, roadside walking, pavements, 12 stiles
Map OS Explorer 129 Yeovil & Sherborne **Grid ref** ST 781135 **Parking** Signposted Sturminster Newton Mill, off A357 just west of Old Town Bridge to south of town

❶ Pass mill and cross bridges, **R** of pond, and through gate into field. Keep **L** up edge (signed 'Colber Bridge'), parallel with Stour. Go through gate and up avenue of trees. Turn **R** along path, then go past playground into Ricketts Lane. Cross high street and turn **R**.

❷ Turn **L** by Old Malt House, to church. Keep **R** of church, and at end of churchyard go through gate, down steps and into lane. This curves **L**. Take path on **R** to Fiddleford Manor and Mill. Go through gate and bear slightly **R** over field, above river. Go through kissing gate and bear **L** along hedge. Continue ahead. At far, **R-H** corner cross 2 footbridges and mill-race, to bear **R**, past mill. Go down drive, turn **R** and **R** again through car park to Fiddleford Manor. Return to lane and turn **R**.

❸ At main road turn **R** then cross to bridleway, going straight uphill into Piddles Wood. At top turn **R** on to track and follow it round hill. Keep forward at 2 fingerposts. Take gate, cross car park; go on **L** to road.

❹ Turn **R** and **L** through farmyard, signed 'Broad Oak'. Go ahead through 2 fields into lane. At end turn **R** along road, and **L** at junction (ignore Donkey Lane **R**). Follow road down, soon bearing **R**. At end of road, take path ahead, and after footbridge turn **L** ('Gipsy's Drove') along bottom of 2 fields to cross stile into woodland.

❺ Turn **R** on unmade lane – Gipsy's Drove. Turn **R** at top of rise on track just before farm. At bottom go through gate and cross field. Cross stile, then go straight on along **R** field edge. Soon cross stile on to path. Bear **R** along hedgerow and cross 2 stiles to lane.

❻ Turn **L** and, in Newton, turn **L** and soon **R** into Hillcrest Close. Where this bends **R**, go down lane. Climb stile (by yellow marker; go down field, with hedge **R**. Leave via gate at bottom, cross A357 and turn **R**. After town sign turn **L** on path 'Newton Farm'. At fingerpost cross stiles and cross field to cross stile **R** of barn; drop through woods. Bear **R** on road then **L** through gate. Cross picnic area to return to car park.

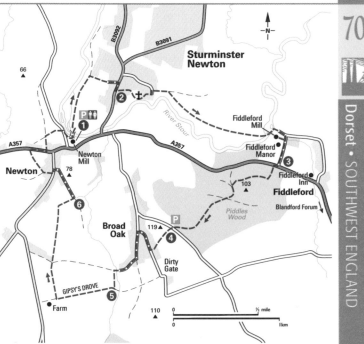

IBBERTON Living On The Edge

From the tops of Bulbarrow Hill to the valley floor and back, via an atmospheric church.

4.25 miles/6.8km 2hrs **Ascent** 591ft/180m ⚠ **Difficulty** 1
Paths Quiet roads, muddy bridleways, field paths, 2 stiles
Map OS Explorer 117 Cerne Abbas & Bere Regis **Grid ref** ST 791071
Parking Car park at Ibberton Hill picnic site

❶ Turn **L** along road, following Wessex Ridgeway, with Ibberton laid out below to **R**. Road climbs gradually, and you see masts on Bulbarrow Hill ahead.
❷ After 1 mile (1.6km) pass car park on **L**, with plaque about Thomas Hardy. At junction bear **R** and immediately **R** again, signposted 'Stoke Wake'. Pass another car park on **R**. Woods of Woolland Hill now fall away steeply on **R**. Pass radio masts to **L** and reach small gate into field on **R**, near end of wood. Before taking it, go extra few steps to road junction ahead for wonderful view of escarpment stretching away west.
❸ Go through gate and follow uneven bridleway down. Glimpse spring-fed lake through trees on **R**. At bottom of field, path swings **L** to gate. Go through, on to road. Turn **R**, continuing downhill. Follow road into Woolland, passing Manor House and Old Schoolhouse, on **L** and **R** respectively.
❹ Beyond entrance, on **L**, to Woolland House turn **R** into lane and immediately **L** through kissing

gate. Path immediately forks. Take **L-H** track, down through marshy patches and young sycamores. Posts with yellow footpath waymarkers lead straight across meadow, with gorse-clad Chitcombe Down up **R**. Cross footbridge over stream. Go straight on to cross road. Keeping straight on, go through hedge gap. Bear **L** down field, cross stile and continue down. Cross footbridge and stile to continue along **L** side of next field. Go through gate to road junction. Walk straight up road ahead and follow it **R**, into Ibberton. Bear **R**.
❺ Continue up this road through village. This steepens and becomes path, bearing **R**. Steps lead up to church. Continue up steep path. Cross road and go straight ahead through gate. Keep straight on along fence, climbing steadily. Cross under power lines, continue in same direction, climbing steadily. Carry on open pasture to small gate in hedge. Do not go through gate, but turn sharp **L**, up slope, to small gate opposite car park.

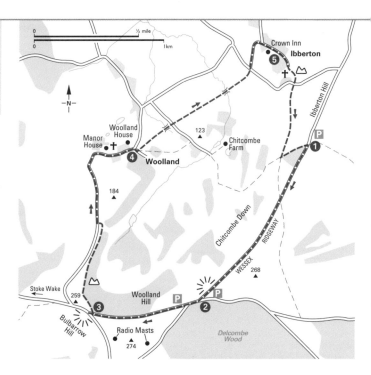

HIGHER MELCOMBE A Lost Village

A hilly rural circuit where, centuries ago, labour economics determined settlement.

5 miles/8km 2hrs 30min **Ascent** 443ft/135m ⚠ **Difficulty** 2
Paths Farmland, woodland track, ancient bridleway, road, 11 stiles
Map OS Explorer 117 Cerne Abbas & Bere Regis **Grid ref** ST 765031
Parking Small parking area on north side of village hall

❶ Turn **L** up road and go immediately **L** down waymarked path. Cross stile, bear down **R** field edge and cross stile at bottom. Continue straight up next field, cross stile and road to go through gate. Keep straight on to reach pair of stiles in hedge.

❷ Cross stiles; bear diagonally across field, in line with farmhouse on skyline; leave by far corner. Keep forward in next field beside hedge, then go through gate, slightly **R** to fingerpost and gate **R** of farmhouse.

❸ Turn **L**, signed 'Dorset Gap', up through farmyard, and take **R-H** of 3 gates. Walk along field edge, above wood. Go through gate and continue straight ahead along ridge top, enjoying superb views over Blackmoor Vale. Track descends abruptly. Turn **R**, through gate, to crossroads of tracks at Dorsetshire Gap.

❹ Turn **L** down bridleway through cleft, signposted 'Higher Melcombe'. Keep straight **R** edge of 2 fields. Ridges and hummocks in field to your **R** are only sign of medieval village. Pass 2 farms at Higher Melcombe, at junction of bridleways, and go through gate and

turn **L**, on to minor road, or walk along avenue that runs alongside (look **R** to see hill track leading to Giant's Grave). Descend past houses to junction.

❺ Turn **L** and walk into Melcombe Bingham. Pass houses then turn **R** before 1st thatched house. Go through gate to take path ahead across field to join fence. Maintain direction up fence, over stile and through woodland. Continue ahead, down field towards Bingham's Melcombe. Cross stile and turn **R**. Follow drive round and down to church.

❻ Retrace route to stile: do not cross but continue up grassy avenue. Before end, turn **L** through gate and go along path. Where this divides keep **L**. Cross stile and follow **R** field edge, then go through gate and descend on track. Go ahead to cross footbridge. Keep straight on, bear **R** over stile in fence and continue down field. Path soon rises up bank and goes along wooded strip to road. Turn **R** to return to car.

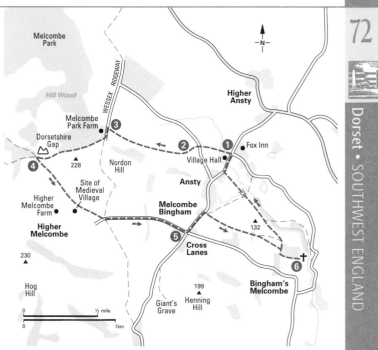

HIGHER BOCKHAMPTON By Hardy's Cottage

Across wooded heath and farmland to where Thomas Hardy, quite literally, left his heart.

5 miles/8km 2hrs **Ascent** 328ft/100m **⚠ Difficulty** ②

Paths Woodland and heathland tracks, muddy field paths and bridleways, firm paths, road, 13 stiles

Map OS Explorer 117 Cerne Abbas & Bere Regis or OL15 Purbeck & South Dorset **Grid ref** SY 725921

Parking Thorncombe Wood (donations) below Hardy's Cottage

❶ Take steep woodland path to **R** of display boards, signposted 'Hardy's Cottage'. Turn **L** at fingerpost and follow winding route down to crossroads of tracks, marked by monument. Turn **L** for Hardy's Cottage.

❷ Retrace route up behind cottage and bear **L**, signed 'Rushy Pond' on path that bears **R**. At crossroads by pond take path ahead signed 'Norris Mill'. Immediately fork **R**; path heads down between fences, soon passing through heathland then between rhododendrons. Cross stile and bear **R**. Enter field by stile and turn **L** up field, towards house.

❸ Cross road to farm track which keeps **R** of barns. Where track ends, bear **R** over field. Cross pair of stiles in hedge; go ahead across fields and drive, passing Duddle Farm (**L**). Cross bridge and stile into field. Go straight on and bear **L**, following track round hill. Cross stile by converted barn and walk up drive. At fingerpost keep straight on through gate. Bear **L** to stile and walk along field edge to gate, then down field

to gate at far corner. Go through and straight on, with river **L**. Go through farmyard and along road.

❹ Turn **L** by Bridge Cottage. Cross river and immediately turn **R**, on to causeway. After 0.5 mile (800m) turn **R**, signed 'Stinsford'. Walk up and turn **L** into churchyard, just below church. Pass church **L**, and Hardy graves **R**. Leave by top gate and walk up road. Pass Casterbridge training centre and turn **R** along road. Take next turn **L** to main road by lodge.

❺ Turn **R**, up road. After entrance to Birkin House, bear **L** through gate and immediately **R** on to path through woodland, parallel with road. Descend, cross stile and bear **L**, 'Higher Bockhampton', and inside field bear diagonally **R** uphill. At top corner keep on through gate and follow fence up to barn. Pass this and take gate on **L**; bear **R** on track to road. Turn **L**, then **R** by postbox, and **R** again to return to car park.

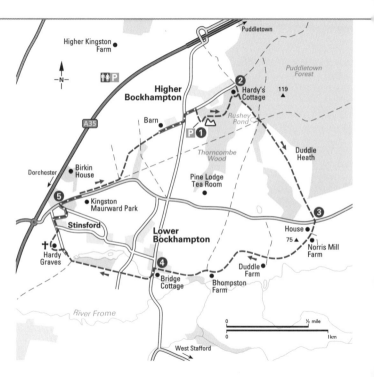

OSMINGTON The White Horse

Osmington's white horse is the only one depicting a rider – King George III.

4 miles/6.4km 2hrs **Ascent** 568ft/173m ⚠ **Difficulty** ☐2

Paths Farm and village lanes, woodland paths, field paths, 7 stiles
Map OS Explorer OL15 Purbeck & South Dorset **Grid ref** SY 724829
Parking Church Lane in Osmington, just off A353

❶ From church walk down street of thatched cottages. At junction keep on down Church Lane. Opposite Cartshed turn **L** up steep steps, signed 'Sutton Poyntz'. Path rises through woodland. After 2nd set of steps path bears **R** and undulates through trees. Cross stile and continue on to end of field.

❷ Cross stile and turn **R** on grass strip between fences, and immediately climb stile on **L**. Cross field in signed direction to stile in far corner. Turn **L** through gate and head straight across field. Cross farm track and bear ahead and **R**. Cross pair of stiles and continue along bottom of field, looking to **R** to see White Horse. Continue though gap. At end of next field take track leading **L** and soon **R** through break in hedge and **R** again. Cross stream and go through small gate. Continue towards Sutton Poyntz, taking gate and then path on to village street.

❸ Turn **R**, pass Mill House and tall, red-brick mill on **L**. Pass village pond and just after Springhead pub on **R**, bear **L** and **R** up lane by Springfield Cottage. Go

through gate with pumping station on **R** and after next stile by gate carry on along track to point, below bottom of steep combe, where spring emerges.

❹ Cross stile by gate and turn **L** up grassy track. Carry on up past beacon on **L**. At top carry on up to gate and junction and turn **R** along fence, signed 'Coastal Path Inland Route', back to Osmington. Pass tumuli, or prehistoric burial mounds. Near ruin, go through gate and keep **L** along field edge. Follow path round to **R** and walk up field and go through small gate to continue along track past trig point. Go through gate and keep straight on.

❺ Go through gate and bear down **R**, signed 'Osmington'. Track leads down hill, through gate – look back to see White Horse again. Follow lane back up through village to your car.

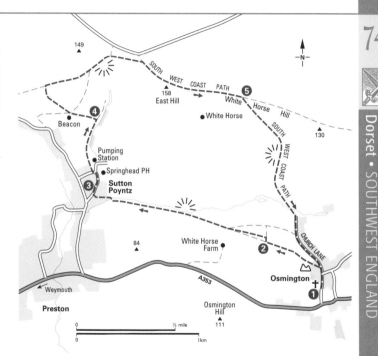

75

PURSE CAUNDLE In The Doghouse

Over hill and down valley from a village dominated by a fine manor house.

5 miles/8km 2hrs **Ascent** 427ft/130m ⚠ **Difficulty** ☐

Paths Muddy field paths, farm tracks, country roads, wet bridleway (wellies recommended), 9 stiles
Map OS Explorer 129 Yeovil & Sherborne **Grid ref** ST 695175
Parking Limited space by church, Purse Caundle

❶ From church walk up street to admire manor house. Return, pass phone box and postbox and turn **L** through gate. Go straight up field edge, cross stile and turn **R** to continue on this line, up through gateway and across another field. After 2nd gateway bear diagonally **R** up field. Cross stile in corner and turn R. Soon cross stile on **R** and pass lake to L. Cross stile at far side and bear **R** along field edge.

❷ Go through gate at corner and go on down field edge. Follow field edge on **R** until you go through gate on **R** by houses, then immediately **L**, up bridleway. This narrows and is shared with stream. Go through gate and keep straight on diagonally **L** up hill. Go through gate in top corner to **L** of where power lines leave field and follow muddy track. This becomes hedged lane; follow to pass Manor Farm.

❸ Turn **L** at fingerpost over stile. Bear **L** down field to cross 2 stiles and footbridge in middle of hedge. Head diagonally **L** down next field. Cross pair of stiles and

footbridge in corner and immediately turn **R** over stile and footbridge. Walk straight ahead up **R** field edge.

❹ At top turn **R**, and take **R-H** of 2 paths (by marker post), along bottom of young plantation. Go throughgateway and turn **L** up field edge. Follow path round behind Frith Farm Cottages, down to gate. Turn **L** on road and walk up it for 0.5 mile (800m), beside wall of Stalbridge Park.

❺ At crossroads turn **L**, towards Frith Farm. Soon bear **R**, following markers. Track then bends **L**, through gate to covered reservoir. Pass this and turn **R**, through gate. Descend steps and bear **L** down field edge, with views to manor. Continue straight on through gap.

❻ At bottom keep forward into woodland. Walk down this ridge, then cross ditch on **L** and turn **R** down edge of field. Go through gateway and retrace route to church.

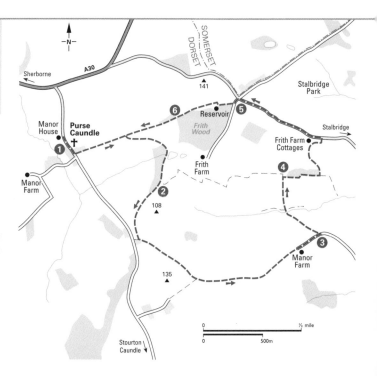

Dorset • SOUTHWEST ENGLAND

SHERBORNE Raleigh's Country Retreat

Around Sherborne, former home of pirate, politician and poet, Sir Walter Raleigh.

6.5 miles/10.4km 3hrs **Ascent** 443ft/135m ⚠ **Difficulty** 1

Paths Country lanes, green lane, field paths, estate tracks, 11 stiles

Map OS Explorer 129 Yeovil & Sherborne **Grid ref** ST 670157

Parking On road by church, Haydon village, 2 miles (3.2km) southeast of Sherborne

1 With church on **L**, walk out of Haydon. At junction continue ahead, signposted 'Bishop's Caundle'. At minor junction cross stile, straight ahead. Turn **R**, up field edge, towards Alweston. Cross stile by fingerpost and bear diagonally **L** over field. Cross stile in corner, go down path and keep straight on down road, which curves past restored pump to meet A3030.

2 Turn **R**, then soon turn **L** over stile in hedge. Go straight over field to gap. Bear diagonally **R** over next field to cross stile just to **R** of where power lines leave field. Continue straight ahead along hedge, crossing stiles and footbridges. Continue along wall towards Folke church. Cross 2 stiles, go through gate and turn **R** up lane into village, passing church entrance and raised pavement on **R**. Keep **L**, by postbox, at junction, then follow lane as it bends round **L**.

3 Follow road as it bends sharply **L** by Pleck Cottage, then turn **R** up signed bridleway. Follow this for 1 mile (1.6km), gently ascending to main road.

4 Turn **L** then **R** through gate directly beside lodge, up lane. Continue straight on down through woods, with park wall **R**. Where drive sweeps **R** by cottage, keep straight on, up track, passing sports fields on **L**. Go through 2 gates, cross road and go through gate by lodge on to tarmac track. Follow this down steep gorge to meet main road. Take path immediately **R**, through gate, and walk up hill above castle gateway.

5 Pass through gate into Sherborne Park. Follow grassy track straight ahead, downhill. Go through kissing gate and ahead on estate track. Go up track to thatched lodge. Here go through gate and up hill.

6 At top keep **R**, through another gate into woods. Follow track round. Keep straight on to tarmac path and pass huge barn on **L**. Follow park road **R**, and go straight on at junction. Descend to lodge. Now go through gate and straight on to return to start.

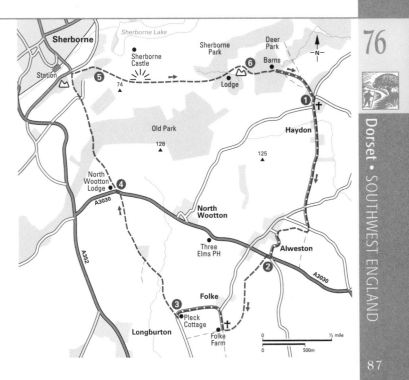

77

CERNE ABBAS Dorset Giant Steps
A valley walk from Minterne Magna to see a famous chalk hill carving.

5.5 miles/8.8km 2hrs 30min **Ascent** 591ft/180m ⚠ **Difficulty** ①
Paths Country paths and tracks, minor road, main road, 5 stiles
Map OS Explorer 117 Cerne Abbas & Bere Regis **Grid ref** ST 659043
Parking Car park (free) opposite church in Minterne Magna

❶ With road behind you, take bridleway on **L** of car park, which soon bends **R** and then **L** round trees, and **L** again on other side. Follow track, keeping **R** at fork, uphill, and where hedge begins pass round to **R** side of it. At top, turn **L** on track inside woods.
❷ Fork **R** through woods. At bottom turn **L** along road. After bend take footpath **R**, across field. After line of trees veer diagonally **L**, towards **R-H** of 2 white gates. Cross road, pass to **R** of this gate, and continue straight down field, with Up Cerne Manor **L**. Pass another white gate to **R** of pond then turn **L** on road. At end bear **R** on to A352.
❸ Soon cross to car park for best view of Giant. Fork **L** on road down to village and turn **L**, signposted 'Village Hall'. Turn **R** by stream, signposted 'Village Centre'. Continue to high street. Turn **L**, and **L** again in front of New Inn, and **L** by Royal Oak, to church. Walk past Old Pitchmarket to Abbey. Turn **R** into churchyard and bear **L**. Go through gate and head **L**.

❹ Cross stile, then turn **R** up steps. Now follow path to **L**, round contour of hill and past National Trust sign for Cerne Giant, below fence. After 0.25 mile (400m), as path divides, keep **R**, up hill, to top. Bear **L** along ridge, cross stile by fingerpost and head diagonally **R**, to another fingerpost.
❺ At fingerpost turn **L**, signed 'Wessex Ridgeway', and go down through gate. Soon turn **R** and follow bridleway along hillside. Keep ahead at junction (signed 'Barne's Lane'), then dip down through gateway and go straight on inside top edge of woods. Keep straight on to go through gate near road. Turn **L** away from road (signed 'Minterne Magna') along **L** edge of large field. At gateway turn **L** on to gravel.
❻ Directly above Minterne House, turn **L** through small gate and signed 'Minterne Magna', towards mast and follow fingerposts to village, down through gates and then along broad track past church to car park.

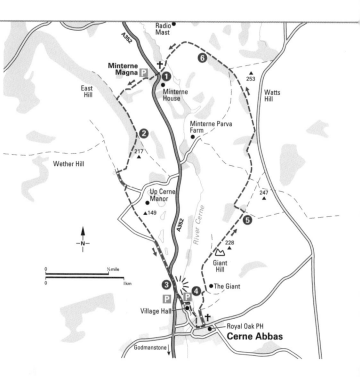

Dorset • SOUTHWEST ENGLAND

88

WINYARD'S GAP The Monarch's Way

A short walk in Dorset's northern uplands following the route of an historic royal escape.

3.25 miles/5.3km 1hr 30min **Ascent** 410ft/125m ▲ **Difficulty** 1
Paths Field paths, some roads, 1 stile
Map OS Explorer 117 Cerne Abbas & Bere Regis **Grid ref** ST 491060
Parking Lay-by north of Cheddington, opposite Court Farm by NT sign for Winyard's Gap

❶ Go through gate at back of lay-by and bear **R** on path up through woods, soon forking **L**. At ridge top turn **L** for memorial. Turn **L** down steps, go back through gate and turn **R** along road. Pass Winyard's Gap Inn on **R** then, at junction, cross straight over and walk up road ahead. Keep **R**, following lane over top of ridge between shoulder-high banks – sign of ancient lane. Flat-topped, bracken-clad Crook Hill is ahead. After 0.5 mile (800m) bear **L** through gate, signposted 'Monarch's Way'.

❷ Bear **R** along top of field, with Chedington Woods falling steeply away **L**, and Crook Hill ahead and R. Go through gate at foot of hill and bear **R** through woods, round base. Cross stile and bear diagonally **L** down field towards **R** of trees. On reaching farm road, turn **R**. Follow it up to meet lane and turn **R**.

❸ After short distance, on corner, go **L** through gate and hook back down fence on bridleway. Go through 2 gates at bottom and continue down field, parallel with top hedge. Twelve Acre Coppice, down to R, is

a lovely stretch of mixed woodland. At bottom cross stream via bridge, then go through gate and straight ahead up track. Go through gate **L** of barn (indicated by blue marker) and turn **R** on farm road, through farmyard. At lane go straight ahead, passing Home Farm on **L**, into hamlet of Weston.

❹ Just before Weston Manor Farm bypass it by turning **R** through gate (blue marker). Turn **L** through gate and turn **R** to resume track straight up hill, with radio mast topping ridge ahead. After short tunnel of trees bear **R** through gate along green track, part of Monarch's Way. Go through gate and stay on track. Go through another gate with ponds down **R**. Soon pass through 2nd gate to **L** of barn, walk past Hunter's Lodge Farm and up drive to road. Turn **R** on main road and follow it back down to inn, with care. Turn **L** here to return to lay-by and car.

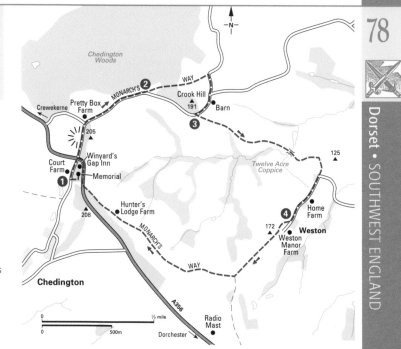

THORNCOMBE Forde Abbey

The going is fairly easy through this area renowned for its soft fruit.

5 miles/8km 2hrs 30min **Ascent** 443ft/135m ⚠ **Difficulty** 1

Paths Field paths, country lanes, 11 stiles **Map** OS Explorer 116 Lyme Regis & Bridport

Grid ref ST 376033 **Parking** By church in Thorncombe village centre

❶ Church **R**; follow road, at 2nd part of churchyard take signposted path on **R** through it. Bear **R** on lane and **L** in front of garages. Cross road by Goose Cottage. Go through gate and follow top of 2 fields, pass barn on **L**, then go straight on down hedge.

❷ Cross corner stile. Cross field. Cross stile; bear diagonally **R**, to corner of next field. Go through gates either side of plank bridge. Cross stream by stone blocks and bear **L**, up field. Cross stile on **L**, and continue up **R**. Soon go through gate and follow path between fences, then through kissing gate and turn **L** along field edge. By trough turn **L** through gate and go ahead up field edge. Enter gate; bear **R**, towards house.

❸ Emerge through gate on to road and turn **L**. At junction turn **R** on to path and head for woods. Turn **L** before edge of woods and, at corner go **R**, through gate. Head diagonally **L** to corner, opposite gates of Forde Abbey. Cross stile and turn **R** on road to cross River Axe.

❹ Soon bear **L** on to footpath and follow it past back of Abbey. At far corner cross footbridge and bear **R**

towards lone cedar; bear **L** up to stile, marked 'Liberty Trail'. Cross; go along top of woods. Soon cross stile and bear diagonally **L** across fields towards another cedar.

❺ Meet road by shed. Go across and up field. (If it is flooded by road, turn **L** on road, and **R** opposite lodge on farm track, bearing **L** at cattle grid by Forde Abbey Farm to reach Point ❻.) Towards top **R-H** corner bear **R** through gate. Keep on this line along top edge. Cross stiles in corner, pass Forde Abbey Farm on **L** and keep straight on by hedge. Cross stile; go down farm road.

❻ At track junction keep straight on. Where track forks bear **L** and head **L** across field. Cross stile in hedge and turn **R** up road. Where copse begins on **R**, take signed footpath on **L**; cross field towards woodland to go through hedge gap. Follow main path through coppice, keeping forward to woodland. Emerge by stile into field, and keep ahead along **L** edge of 2 fields. Halfway into 3rd field, where houses begin, go **L** through gate and **R** on enclosed path to Thorncombe and passing playground. Turn **L** on village street to church.

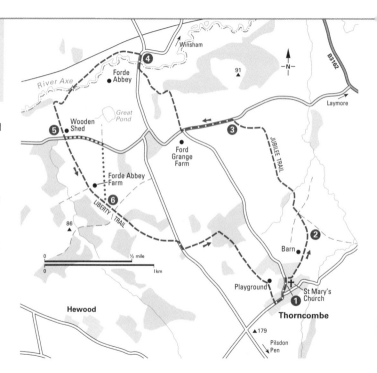

SEATOWN Golden Cap In Trust

Climb a fine top, owned by one of the country's most popular charities.

4 miles/6.4km 2hrs 30min **Ascent** 1,007ft/307m ⚠ **Difficulty** ②
Paths Field tracks, country lanes, steep zig-zag gravel path, 5 stiles
Map OS Explorer 116 Lyme Regis & Bridport **Grid ref** SY 420917
Parking Car park (charge) above gravel beach in Seatown; beware, can flood in stormy weather

❶ Walk back up through Seatown. Cross stile on **L**, on to footpath, signposted 'Coast Path Diversion'. Cross stile at end, carry on across field to cross stile and footbridge into woodland. Cross stile at other side and bear **R** up hill, signposted 'Golden Cap'.

❷ Where track forks by bench keep **L**. Go through trees and over stile. Bear **L**, straight across open hillside, with Golden Cap ahead. Pass through line of trees and walk up fence. Go up steps, cross stile and continue ahead. At fingerpost go **L** through gate to follow path of shallow steps up through bracken, heather, bilberry and bramble to top of Golden Cap.

❸ Pass trig point and turn **R** along top. Pass stone memorial to Earl of Antrim. At marker stone turn **R** and follow zig-zag path steeply downhill, enjoying great views. Go through gate and bear **R** over field towards ruined St Gabriel's Chapel. In bottom corner turn down through gate, passing ruins on R, then go through 2nd gate. Go downtrack, passing cottages on **L**, and bear **R** up farm road, signed 'Morcombelake'.

Follow this up between high banks and hedges. Continue through gateway.

❹ At road junction, turn **R** down Muddyford Lane, signed 'Langdon Hill'. Pass gate of Shedbush Farm and continue straight up hill. Turn **R** up concreted lane towards Filcombe Farm. Follow blue markers through farmyard, bearing **L** through 2 gates. Walk up track, go along **R** edge of 1st field and across next field. Head **L** over top of green saddle between Langdon Hill and Golden Cap.

❺ Go **L** through gate in corner and down track (Pettycrate Lane) beside woods, signed 'Seatown'. Ignore footpath over stile to **R**. At junction of tracks keep **R**, downhill. Pass Seahill House on **L** and turn **R**, on to road. Continue down road into Seatown village to return to car.

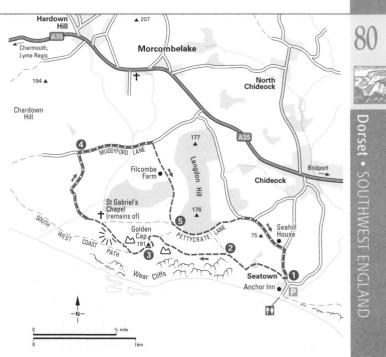

GREAT BEDWYN A Working Windmill

A peaceful canal walk, visiting Wiltshire's only working windmill.

6.75 miles/10.9km 2hrs **Ascent** 147ft/45m ▲ **Difficulty** 1

Paths Field paths, woodland tracks, towpath, roads, 3 stiles

Map OS Explorer 157 Marlborough & Savernake Forest **Grid ref** SU 279645

Parking Great Bedwyn Station

1 Walk to main road in Great Bedwyn. Turn **R**, then **L** down Church Street. Pass Lloyd's Stone Museum and church, then take footpath **L** between 2 graveyards. Climb stile, cross field to kissing gate, then carefully cross railway line to another kissing gate. Cross footbridge, then bridge over Kennet and Avon Canal and descend to towpath.

2 Turn **R**, pass beneath bridge and continue along towpath for 1.5 miles (2.4km), passing 3 locks and 2 stiles, to reach Lock 60. Cross canal here, turn **L**, then follow path **R** and pass through tunnel beneath railway. Ascend steps to Crofton Pumping Station.

3 Retrace steps back to towpath and Lock 60. Turn **L** for few paces, then take footpath R, waymarked to Wilton Windmill, and walk beside Wilton Water along edge of fields. Eventually, turn **R** down short track to lane by village pond in Wilton.

4 Turn **L**, then just past Swan Inn, follow lane **L** and uphill through trees. Climb out of village and fork **R** to

pass Wilton Windmill. Continue along lane and turn **L** on to track, opposite lane to Hungerford. Just before wooded track snakes downhill, turn **R** along bridle path (unsigned) beside woodland.

5 At staggered crossing of paths, turn **R**, then in 50yds (46m), turn **L**. Go down well-surfaced track and through gate into Bedwyn Brail. Continue though woods, following signs to Great Bedwyn. Go straight across clearing before forking **L** to re-enter woods in the **L-H** corner of clearing.

6 On emerging in field corner, keep **L** along field boundary. Go through gap in hedge and descend along **L-H** side of next field, with Great Bedwyn visible ahead. Near bottom of field, bear half **R**, downhill to canal.

7 Pass through gate by bridge and Lock 64 and turn **R** along towpath. Go through car park to road, then turn **L** over canal and rail bridges before turning **R** back to Great Bedwyn Station.

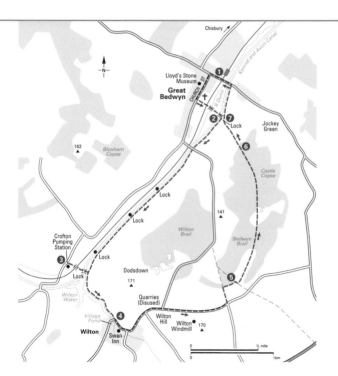

SAVERNAKE A Royal Forest

Through an ancient forest landscape high above Marlborough.

9 miles/14.5km 3hrs 30min **Ascent** 213ft/65m ⚠ **Difficulty** ☐ 1
Paths Woodland tracks, towpath, bridle paths, country lanes, 10 stiles
Map OS Explorer 157 Marlborough & Savernake Forest **Grid ref** SU 215646
Parking Hat Gate 8 picnic area off A346 south of Marlborough

❶ From car park, turn R, then almost immediately L past wooden barrier. Follow wooded path for 500yds (457m), then bear R to reach A346. Cross near old milestone and take track beyond wooden barrier (signed 'Tottenham House').

❷ In 150yds (137m), at major crossing, turn R and, after similar distance, keep L at junction where path runs straight on. Follow track (which can be very muddy) for 0.75 mile (1.2km) to The Column.

❸ Approaching it, turn L and follow track to junction with Grand Avenue. Turn R and follow it to road. Turn L, pass Warren Lodge and take next R turning for St Katharine's Church.

❹ Beyond church turn R at sign for Durley. Pass through trees and beyond gate, bear R to drive, crossing it to stile beyond woodland. Cross parkland and woodland and drive to Tottenham House and continue to road.

❺ Turn L, walk through Durley and keep to lane across old railway bridge, then main railway bridge,

and shortly take footpath on R, waymarked 'Wootton Rivers'. You are now walking above the Kennet and Avon Canal as it passes through the Bruce Tunnel.

❻ Walk down steps, pass through narrow and low tunnel under railway line and join canal towpath just below entrance to Bruce Tunnel. Turn L along towpath for 1.5 miles (2.4km), passing beneath A346 at Burbage Wharf to reach Cadley Lock.

❼ Turn R over bridge No 105 and follow metalled track to T-junction. Turn R and keep to road, passing 2 dismantled railway bridges, back to car park at Hat Gate.

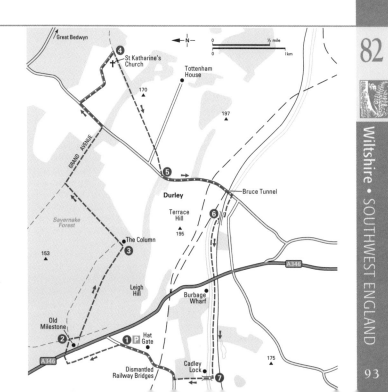

DOWNTON Admiral Lord Nelson
Discover an 18th-century estate associated with Lord Nelson.

5 miles/8km 2hrs 30min **Ascent** 229ft/70m ⚠ **Difficulty** ①
Paths Riverside paths, downland tracks, metalled lanes, 5 stiles
Map OS Explorers 130 Salisbury & Stonehenge; 131 Romsey, Andover & Test Valley **Grid ref** SU 180214
Parking Plenty of roadside parking in High Street

❶ Head west along High Street, cross river bridge and take footpath **R**, signed 'Charlton All Saints'. Walk alongside river, go through kissing gate and keep to footpath as it swings away from river along causeway through water-meadows. When path widens and bears **L**, fork **R** to stile and footbridge.

❷ Turn **R** along concrete track then, as it bears **L** towards farm buildings, fork **R** through kissing-gate and keep to **R-H** field edge to small brick bridge and kissing-gate. Now cross 2 fields to kissing gate by house. Cross gravel drive and stile opposite. Walk beside hedge on **R**, following it **L,** then continue ahead to public footbridge.

❸ Cross stile and footbridge, and walk through reedy marshland. Pass through old gateway and then cross footbridges to reach mill. Turn **L** in front of mill and follow concrete driveway. In 100yds (91m), take waymarked footpath sharp **L** (bear **R** to chapel), uphill through woodland, eventually reaching fork.

❹ Take main path **R** to stile on woodland edge. Bear half **R** across field to gate (Trafalgar House is on **R**), and follow woodland path for 0.25 mile (400m) to lane. Turn **R** uphill, then **L** at junction opposite lodge.

❺ Cross bridge over disused railway and take arrowed bridle path **R**). Continue beside old railway, following **R-H** edge of 2 fields to road.

❻ Turn **R** under bridge, then **L** to follow old embankment. When this peters out, maintain direction over hill and descend to cross path.

❼ Descend into valley and, as you start to ascend, take path to **R** of embankment. At top of rise, turn **L** over stile and continue beside old railway. Cross stile and keep ahead along enclosed path to residential road. Keep ahead for 50yds (46m) and turn **R** down signposted path to gate. Walk down drive and turn **L** back to High Street.

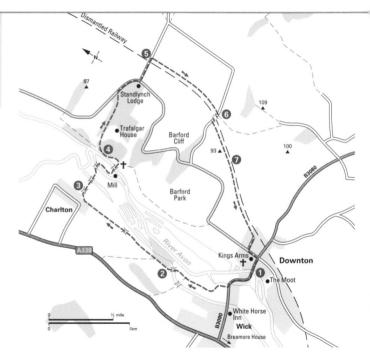

AMESBURY Glimpses Of Stonehenge
A downland and riverside ramble.

6.5 miles/10.4km 3hrs **Ascent** 518ft/158m ⚠ **Difficulty** 2
Paths Tracks, field and bridle paths, roads, 2 stiles
Map OS Explorer 130 Salisbury & Stonehenge **Grid ref** SU 149411
Parking Free parking at Amesbury Recreation Ground car park

❶ Take footpath to **R** of play area, cross footbridge; bear **R** to cross main footbridge over River Avon. At crossing of tracks, take track signed 'Durnford', passing **R** of cottages. Head uphill to junction and go straight on, downhill to gate. Turn **R** along field edge and bear **L** in corner to join path that passes through valley bottom beside stream to shortly cross footbridge on **R**.
❷ Follow path through marshy ground to cross bridge over Avon. Bear **R** over bridge and keep **L** through paddock beside cob wall of Normanton Down House to stile. Bear **R** along fenced path beside drive to road. Turn **L** then reach **R** turn.
❸ Walk up tarmac road towards Springbottom Farm or join path through spinney on **R** for views to Stonehenge. Pass covered reservoir and barns, then descend to farm complex. Just beyond barns, bear **L** with red byway arrow on to track beside paddocks.
❹ Keep to track through valley (Lake Bottom) for 1 mile (1.6km). Where it is metalled take arrowed path **R**, between fences, into woodland and bear **L** uphill.

Out of trees, keep **R** along field edge to stile.
❺ Cross lane and take bridlepath **R** in front of thatched house. Go past (not through) gap **L**, to descend gently. Cross drive and bear **L** to cross 2 footbridges over Avon. Pass beside Durnford Mill and follow drive out to lane.
❻ Turn **L** through Great Durnford, passing church and drive to Great Durnford Manor, following public road **R**, uphill through woodland. Descend and take waymarked bridle path **L** beside Fairwood House.
❼ Ascend by edge of Ham Wood. Leaving wood, do not curve **L** and down; pare **R** along path to gate. Keep **R** along 2 fenced field edges to gate.
❽ Maintain direction through pastureland, not losing height, eventually easing **R** towards field boundary corner. Continue for 0.25 mile (400m), following field edge. Keeping this line, descend field edge to gate to rejoin outward route. Retrace steps to car park.

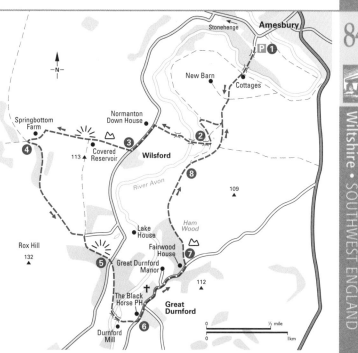

PITTON Clarendon's Lost Palace

Exploring ancient woodland for the remains of Clarendon Palace.

7.5 miles/12.1km 3hrs **Ascent** 410ft/125m ⚠ **Difficulty** 1

Paths Field paths, woodland tracks, country lanes, 10 stiles

Map OS Explorers 131 Romsey, Andover & Test Valley and 130 Salisbury & Stonehenge

Grid ref SU 212312 (on Explorer 131) **Parking** Pitton village hall. Considerate roadside parking in Pitton

❶ Locate The Silver Plough pub and walk up cul-de-sac **R** of it. In 100yds (91m), take footpath **R**, heading uphill between houses to stile. Proceed across narrow field to stile, then go ahead along **R-H** field edge to gap.

❷ Cross track and continue along another track to **R** of woodland. It narrows and soon reaches stile. Keep ahead to enter Church Copse. Where fenced path joins track bear **R** then, at junction on woodland fringe, keep straight on downhill into Farley village.

❸ At road, turn **R** and pass All Saints Church and almshouses. Leave village and take 2nd path on **L** (1st has coronation tree and plaque). Go diagonally **R** and follow hedge **R** to stile by bungalow. Walk down drive, cross lane to gate and follow path through long field to stile and gate.

❹ Proceed across next field (**L** of power cables) to stile and gate. Take track immediately **R** and follow this byway to track T-junction with footpath into field on **R**.

Turn **L** alongside fenced enclosure and, on emerging from wood, head straight across 2 fields and enter more woodland.

❺ Walk through woodland alongside clearing to **R**, and cross lane back into woodland. Leave wood and follow track **R**, then **L** around field edge and soon re-enter wood. Keep ahead where Clarendon Way merges from **R** and continue to ruins of Clarendon Palace.

❻ From palace remains, retrace steps through wood, this time keeping **L** along Clarendon Way. Follow path for nearly 1 mile (1.6km) through wood. On emerging, keep straight on down track and cross lane by barn.

❼ Pass beside white cottages and woodland to **R**, then walk down fenced path, soon to follow diverted footpath signs to sewage pumping station. At lane turn **L**, then **R**, back to start.

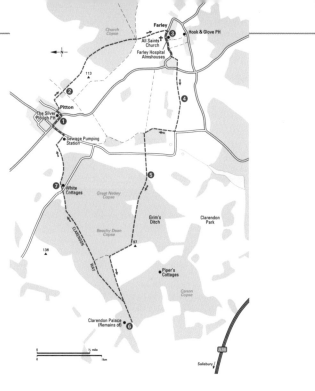

SALISBURY A Historic Trail
Around a cathedral city.

3 miles/4.8km 2hrs (longer if visiting attractions) **Ascent** Negligible ⚠ **Difficulty** 1
Paths Pavements and metalled footpaths
Map OS Explorer 130 Salisbury & Stonehenge; AA Street by Street Salisbury **Grid ref** SU 141303
Parking Central car park (signed off A36 Ring Road)

❶ Join Riverside Walk and follow signposted path through Maltings Shopping Centre towards St Thomas's church. On reaching St Thomas's Square, close to the Polly Tearooms, bear **R** to junction of Bridge Street, Silver Street and High Street.

❷ Turn **L** along Silver Street and cross road to Poultry Cross. Keep ahead along Butcher Row and Fish Row to pass Guildhall and tourist information centre. Turn **R** along Queen Street and turn **R** along New Canal to view cinema foyer.

❸ Return to crossroads and continue ahead along Milford Street to pass Red Lion. Turn **R** along Brown Street, then **L** along Trinity Street to pass Trinity Hospital. Pass Love Lane into Barnard Street and follow road **R** to reach Joiners' Hall.

❹ Walk down St Ann Street and keep ahead on merging with Brown Street to reach T-junction with St John's Street. Cross over and go through St Ann Gate into Cathedral Close. Pass Malmesbury House and Bishops Walk and take path diagonally **L** across green

to reach main entrance to cathedral.

❺ Pass entrance, walk beside barrier ahead and turn R. Shortly, turn **R** again along West Walk, passing Salisbury and South Wiltshire Museum and Military Museum. Keep ahead around Chorister Green to pass Mompesson House.

❻ Bear **L** through gates into High Street and turn **L** at crossroads along Crane Street. Cross River Avon and turn **L** along metalled path beside river through Queen Elizabeth Gardens. Keep **L** by play area and soon cross footbridge to follow Town Path across water-meadows to Old Mill (hotel) in Harnham.

❼ Return along Town Path, cross footbridge and keep ahead to Crane Bridge Road. Bear R, recross Avon and turn immediately **L** along riverside path to Bridge Street. Cross straight over and follow path ahead towards The Mill. Walk back through Maltings Shopping Centre to car park.

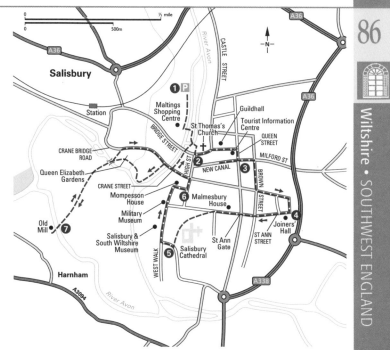

LYDIARD PARK Swindon's Surprise

A rural ramble from a Palladian mansion and country park on Swindon's urban fringe.

2.5 miles/4km 1hr **Ascent** 65ft/20m ⚠ **Difficulty** ☐1

Paths Well-defined parkland paths and tracks, one stretch of quiet road

Map OS Explorer 169 Cirencester & Swindon **Grid ref** SU 101844

Parking Free parking at Lydiard Country Park

❶ Turn **L** out of car park, pass Forest Café and continue along track to Lydiard House and church. With church on **R**, bear **L** through car park, ignoring gate on **R**, and go through another gate. Walk beside walled garden and follow path **L** into woodland.

❷ Just before small clearing, turn **R** signposted 'Lydiard Millicent and Purton' to reach gate on woodland edge. Proceed ahead across field on defined path to bridge spanning stream.

❸ Pass beneath electricity cables and turn **L** at junction signposted 'West Park Circuit'. Follow straight path with plantations to **R** and at next junction, with path to Lydiard Millicent on **R**, turn **L** on path marked 'West Park Circuit'.

❹ Keep woodland **R** and follow broad track. Go through gates and continue ahead, avoiding **L-H** path back to Lydiard House on **L**. Keep ahead with hedgerow and trees to **R** and at 1st field corner bear **R** to road at Hook Street.

❺ Turn **L**, follow narrow lane between fields and trees, pass under cables again and avoid stile and footpath on **R**. Turn **L** for few paces and through galvanised kissing gate.

❻ Bear **R**, following field edge, and make for copse. Pass alongside it to reach gate. Just beyond it turn **L** onto path running alongside wire fencing. Follow across long rectangular pasture and swing **R** with field boundary. Merge with clearly defined track, with Lydiard House seen ahead framed by trees. Head for clearing and retrace steps back to country park and car park.

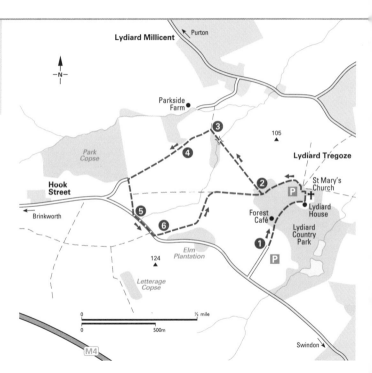

GREAT WISHFORD Grovely Wood

Learn all about Wiltshire's oldest-surviving custom on this peaceful walk through ancient Grovely Wood.

5 miles/8km 2hrs 30min **Ascent** 370ft/113m ⚠ **Difficulty** 2
Paths Woodland paths and downland tracks **Map** OS Explorer 130 Salisbury & Stonehenge
Grid ref SU 080353 **Parking** Roadside parking in South Street, Great Wishford

1 Head along South Street to church and turn **L** at T-junction. Walk past Royal Oak. Go under railway bridge and immediately turn **R** to walk along waymarked bridle path beside cemetery. Ascend track to gate.

2 Walk along **L-H** field edge to gate, continue beside trees and bear **R** around top of field making for opening that leads into woodland. Turn almost immediately **L** along woodland track, following it for some distance to T-junction. Turn **R** up metalled lane.

3 At first major junction, by patch of grass, turn **L** and then **L** again to follow track running down broad beech avenue (First Broad Drive) along course of Roman road, or Lead Road, which traversed Wessex from lead mines of Mendips in Somerset to join other ancient routes at Old Sarum, such as Harrow Way to Kent. You are now walking through Grovely Wood, a fine stretch of woodland that was once a royal hunting forest and which, together with the New Forest and Cranborne Chase, formed a very significant preserve.

4 After 1 mile (1.6km), at crossing of public bridle paths, turn **L** and keep to main track downhill through woodland, ignoring all cross paths and forks. Emerge from Grovely Wood and follow track downhill towards Great Wishford. Pass beneath railway line to lane. Turn **L**, then fork **R** along South Street.

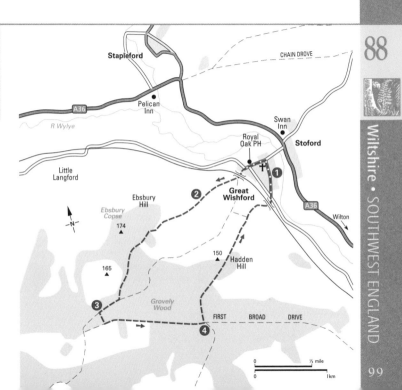

AVEBURY Pagan Pastures

Explore the famous stone circle and some fine prehistoric monuments.

5 miles/8km 2hrs 30min **Ascent** 262ft/80m ▲ **Difficulty** 2
Paths Tracks, field paths, some road walking, 4 stiles
Map OS Explorer 157 Marlborough & Savernake Forest **Grid ref** SU 099696
Parking Large National Trust car park in Avebury

❶ From car park, walk to main road and turn **R**. In 50yds (46m), cross and go through gate with blue bridleway sign. Pass through another gate and follow path alongside river. Go through 2 more gates and cross 2 stiles, passing Silbury Hill.

❷ Beyond gate, walk down **R-H** field edge to gate and A4. Cross and turn **L**, then almost immediately **R** through gate. Walk down gravel track and cross bridge over stream. Track soon narrows to footpath. Go through kissing gate and turn sharp **L**.

❸ To visit West Kennett Long Barrow, shortly turn **R**. Otherwise go straight on around the **L-H** field edge to stile and continue along track. At staggered junction, keep ahead across stile and walk along **R-H** field boundary. Keep to **R** in corner by redundant stile and cross stile on **R** in next corner and proceed up narrow footpath.

❹ At T-junction, go **L** and descend to road. Turn **L**, then just beyond bridge, take bridle path sharp **R**.

Follow **R-H** field edge to gap in corner and turn sharp **L** following track uphill. At top you'll see tumuli on **R** and The Sanctuary on **L**. Continue to A4.

❺ Cross A4 and head up Ridgeway. After 500yds (457m), turn **L** off Ridgeway on to byway. Bear half **R** by clump of trees on tumuli and keep to established track, eventually reaching T-junction by farm buildings, Manor Farm.

❻ Turn **L**, signed 'Avebury', and follow metalled track through earthwork and straight over staggered crossroads by Red Lion Inn. Turn **L** opposite National Trust signpost and walk back to car park.

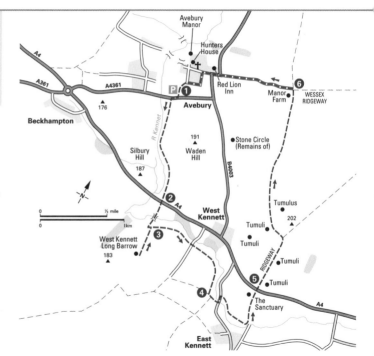

CRICKLADE The Infant Thames

An easy ramble across water-meadows.

5.5 miles/8.8km 2hrs 30min **Ascent** Negligible ⚠ **Difficulty** 1

Paths Field paths and bridle paths, disued railway, town streets, 6 stiles

Map OS Explorer 169 Cirencester & Swindon **Grid ref** SU 100934

Parking Cricklade Town Hall car park (free)

❶ Turn **R** out of car park, keep ahead at roundabout and walk along High Street. Pass St Mary's Church, then turn **L** along North Wall before river bridge. Shortly, bear **R** to gate and join Thames Path. Keep on this route, walking along field edge to reach houses.
❷ Go through kissing gate on **R** and bear **L** across field to gate. Follow fenced footpath, cross plank bridge and pass through gate immediately on **R**. Cross river bridge and turn **L** through gate. Walk beside infant Thames, crossing 2 gates into North Meadow.
❸ Continue and cross stile by bridge. Go through gate immediately **R** and keep straight ahead, ignoring the Thames Path, **L**. Follow path beside disused canal. Cross footbridge and stile then, at fence, bear **R** to cross footbridge close to house named The Basin. Bear **R** along drive.
❹ Cross bridge and turn **L** through gateway. Shortly, bear **R** to join path along **L** side of old canal. Keep to path for 0.5 mile (800m) to road. Turn **L** into Cerney Wick to reach T-junction.

❺ Cross stone stile opposite and keep ahead through paddock to stone stile and lane. Cross lane and go through gate opposite, continuing ahead to kissing gate and stile. Follow the path ahead. Bear **R**, then **L** and bear off **L** (yellow arrow) into trees.
❻ Cross footbridge and proceed ahead along field edge to stile. Turn **L** along old railway, signed 'Cricklade'. Cross River Thames in 1 mile (1.6km) and keep to path along former trackbed to reach bridge.
❼ Follow gravel path to Leisure Centre. Bear **L** on to road, following it **R**, then turn **L** opposite entrance to Leisure Centre car park. Turn **R**, then next **L** and follow road to church (St Sampsons).
❽ Walk beside barrier and turn **R** in front of The Gatehouse into churchyard. Bear **L** to main gates and follow lane to T-junction. Turn **R** to return to car park.

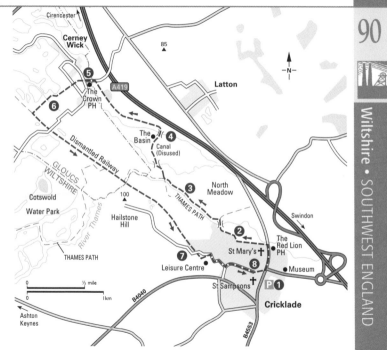

WARDOUR Old And New Castles
Rolling parkland around medieval ruins.

3.75 miles/6km 1hr 45min **Ascent** 278ft/85m **⚠ Difficulty** ☐1

Paths Field and woodland paths, parkland tracks, 11 stiles
Map OS Explorer 118 Shaftesbury & Cranborne Chase **Grid ref** ST 938264
Parking Free parking at Old Wardour Castle

❶ From parking area, turn **L** along drive and pass between castle and Cresswell's Pond. Pass Gothic Pavilion, then at Wardour House (private) bear **R** with trackway. Gently climb wide track, skirting woodland, then at fork keep **R**. At end of woodland, cross stile by field entrance and walk ahead along **R-H** side of field, heading downhill to stile.

❷ Follow path beside Pale Park Pond to squeeze gate, then ascend across field to further squeeze gate into woodland. Shortly, bear **R** to continue along main forest track, before leaving Wardour Wood beside gate on to gravel drive.

❸ At end of drive, cross stile on **R**. Head downhill across field to metal gate and follow waymarked path through Park Copse, soon to bear **L** down grassy clearing to squeeze gate beside field entrance. Follow R-H edge towards Park Gate Farm.

❹ Cross stile on to farm drive and turn **R** (yellow arrow) to cross concrete farmyard to gate. Follow path

beside hedge to further gate, with River Nadder on **L**, then proceed ahead along **R-H** field edge to double stile in far corner. Bear diagonally **L** across field, aiming for **L-H** side of cottage. Go through gate and maintain direction to stile.

❺ Cross farm drive and stile opposite and head straight uphill, keeping **L** of tree, towards stile and woodland. Follow path **R** through trees and soon bear **L** to pas building on **L**. New Wardour Castle is visible **R**. Keep close to bushes across grounds towards main drive and turn **R** along gravel path.

❻ Join drive and walk past New Wardour Castle. Where track forks, keep **R** to stile beside gate. Follow track ahead across parkland towards Old Wardour Castle. Climb stile beside gate and proceed ahead, following track uphill to T-junction of tracks. Turn **L** and follow your outward route back to car park.

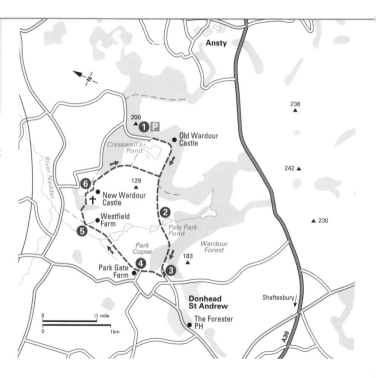

CALNE Exploring Bowood Park

A visit to one of Wiltshire's grandest houses.

7 miles/11.3km 3hrs 30min **Ascent** 360ft/110m ⚠ **Difficulty** [2]
Paths Field, woodland and parkland paths, metalled drives, pavement beside A4, former railway line, 3 stiles **Map** OS Explorer 156 Chippenham & Bradford-on-Avon **Grid ref** ST 998710
Parking Choice of car parks in Calne

❶ Find library on The Strand (A4); head south along New Road to roundabout. Turn **R** along Station Road and take footpath **L** opposite fire station. Turn **C** on Wenhill Lane and follow it out of built-up area.
❷ Nearing cottage, follow waymark **L** and along field edge. Beyond cottage, climb bank and keep **L** along field edge to plank bridge and stile. Keep to **L-H** field edge; soon bear **L** to stile. Follow path R, through rough grass around Pinhills Farm to stile opposite bungalow and turn **L** along drive.
❸ At junction, turn sharp **R** along drive and continue for 1 mile (1.6km). Near bridge, take footpath **R**, through kissing gate; go through parkland beside pond. Cross bridge, go through gate and turn **R** alongside Bowood Lake.
❹ Bowood House ahead, bear **L** to gate and cross causeway to gate. Keep straight on up track, following it **L** and then **R** to cross driveway to Bowood House.
❺ Beyond gate, keep ahead along field edge, soon follow path **L** across Bowood Park. Keep **L** of trees

and field boundary to gate. Turn **R** along drive beside Bowood Golf Course. Where drive turns sharp **R** to cottage, keep on into woodland.
❻ Swing immediately **R**, then follow path **L**, downhill through clearing (can be boggy) along telegraph poles. Turn **L** at bottom of hill and follow woodland path uphill beside golf course. Turn **R** through break in trees and go through main gates to Bowood House into Derry Hill.
❼ Turn **R** along Old Road. At A4, turn **R** along pavement. Soon cross to opposite pavement and continue downhill. Pass under footbridge; take drive **R**.
❽ Join former railway line at Black Dog Halt. Turn **L** and follow this towards Calne. Cross disused canal and turn **R** along towpath. Where path forks keep **R** to Station Road. Retrace your steps to start.

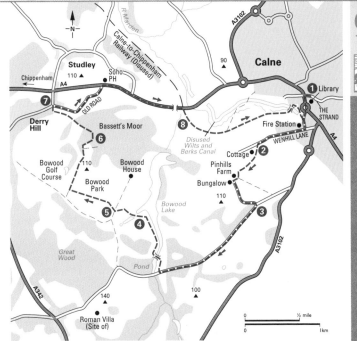

92

Wiltshire • SOUTHWEST ENGLAND

103

BREMHILL Maud Heath's Causeway

Follow field paths to a hilltop monument and the start of Maud Heath's Causeway.

4 miles/6.4km 1hr 30min **Ascent** 295ft /90m ⚠ **Difficulty** 2

Paths Field paths, bridle paths, metalled roads, 10 stiles
Map OS Explorer 156 Chippenham & Bradford-on-Avon **Grid ref** ST 980730
Parking Bremhill church

❶ With your back to church, turn **R** and walk downhill through Bremhill. Begin to climb and take arrowed path **L** to go through gate. Proceed straight on below bank along field edge to opening in corner. Bear diagonally **R**, heading uphill through 2 fields to lane.

❷ Cross stile opposite and cross paddock to next stile. Bear slightly **L** to stile in field corner and walk along **L-H** edge to gate and stile and maintain direction to stile. In next field look out for and pass through gate on **L** and head straight across field to gate and lane.

❸ Turn **L**, then immediately bear **R** to gate. Join waymarked bridle path along **R-H** field edge to gate. Maintain direction through several fields and gates to monument to Maud Heath on top of Wick Hill.

❹ Continue to cross lane via gates, passing stone tablet and inscription identifying beginning of Maud Heath's Causeway. Follow bridle path along crest

of hill through 7 fields via gates and bear **L** before woodland to reach gate and lane at top of Bencroft Hill.

❺ Turn **L**, pass Bencroft Farm and bungalow, then take waymarked path **R**, through woodland bearing **L** on nearing gate to cross stile. Proceed straight across field on defined path, cross stile and remain on path to stile to **L** of bungalow.

❻ Turn **L** along lane, heading uphill to junction beside Dumb Post Inn. Turn **R**, then **L** along drive to thatched cottage. Go through squeeze stile and keep to **L-H** edge of field through gate and squeeze stile to reach stile in field corner. Walk in front of Manor Farm to reach gate leading into Bremhill churchyard. Bear **R** along path back to car.

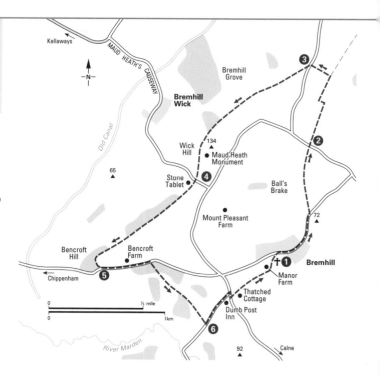

HEYTESBURY The Chalk Stream

A gentle stroll along the River Wylye.

4 miles/6.4km 2hrs **Ascent** 49ft/15m ⚠ **Difficulty** ☐1

Paths Field paths and bridleways, 9 stiles

Map OS Explorer 143 Warminster & Trowbridge **Grid ref** ST 926425

Parking Plenty of room along wide village street

❶ Head east along village street, pass Angel Inn and turn **R** down Mantles Lane. Where it curves **R** to become Mill Street, take footpath **L** along drive beside River Wylye. Bear **R** on to footpath in front of Mantles Cottage, go through kissing gate and walk along **R-H** edge of pasture, soon to bear slightly **L** on nearing Mill Farm to reach gate.

❷ Beyond next gate, turn **R** across bridge, then follow indistinct yellow arrow **L** and soon cross footbridge. Fork **L** at junction of ways then, just before further footbridge, turn **L** through gap and bear **R** along field edge. At yellow arrow, bear half **L** across field towards thatched cottages to riverbank and bear **R** to stile and junction of paths.

❸ Turn **L** across footbridge, pass Knook Manor and St Margaret's Church, then turn **R** by post-box and soon pass East Farm on track (messy after rain). At 2 gates, go through **L-H** gate and proceed ahead along **R-H** field edge to another gate. Continue on into Upton Lovell.

❹ At crossroads, take signed footpath **R**, then just before drive to Hatch House, follow path **L** to footbridge over river. Go through gate and proceed ahead along field edge to gate. Turn **L** through kissing gate, walk along hedged path and cross railway with great care via gates and steps. Continue to lane in Corton.

❺ Turn **L** through village, eventually passing Dove Inn. At T-junction, take arrowed path across stile on **R**. Head across field on defined path to stile and keep ahead through gate to further stile. Go along **R-H** edge of field and shortly, climb stile, turn **L** along field edge to stile and pass beneath railway.

❻ Cross stile and walk beside **R-H** fence to gate. From here, follow track ahead. Cross another stile and keep to track until you reach lane. Turn **R** and follow it through buildings at Mill Farm and across river to rejoin outward route beside river back into Heytesbury.

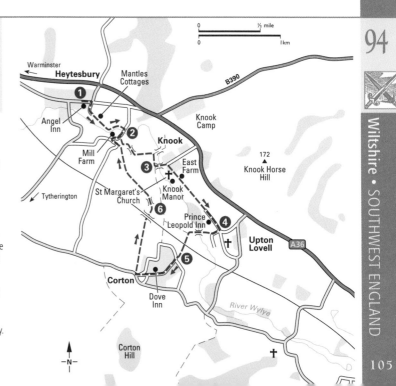

FONTHILL Fantastic Folly

Explore Fonthill Park, ridge-top woodlands and pastures around Fonthill Bishop.

4.25 miles/6.8km 2hrs **Ascent** 278ft/85m ⚠ **Difficulty** 1

Paths Tracks, field and woodland paths, parkland, some road walking
Map OS Explorer 143 Warminster & Trowbridge **Grid ref** ST 933316
Parking Lay-by close to southern end of Fonthill Lake

1 With your back to lay-by, turn **R** along road (can be busy) that traverses Fonthill Park beside lake for just over 0.5 mile (800m). Pass beneath magnificent stone arch and shortly bear **R** to B3089. Keep to **R** along pavement into pretty village of Fonthill Bishop.
2 Turn **R** just beyond bus shelter on to metalled track. After few paces, turn **L** onto waymarked bridleway through Old Dairy. Keep **L**, and join track that winds uphill towards woodland. Follow grassy track beside Fonthill Clump and keep to main track above valley. In 0.5 mile (800m) fork **R** downhill into Little Ridge Wood.
3 At T-junction, turn **L** and keep **L** at next 2 junctions, following wide path to gate and lane. Turn **R** through hamlet of Ridge. Pass telephone box, walk uphill and bear off R, following signposted footpath along drive to Fonthill House.
4 In 0.25 mile (400m), fork **L** with footpath sign to follow track between paddocks and through gateway.

In 200yds (183m), fork **R** with yellow arrow and walk beside woodland. On entering open field, turn **L** along field edge, turning **R** at corner and keeping hedge on **L** to gradually descend towards woodland.
5 Enter wood and bear **L**, then **R** along gravel track beside Fonthill Lake. Cross weir to town. Disregard track which goes ahead uphill and bear off **R** along lakeside edge. Follow well-established path through gate, eventually returning to parking area.

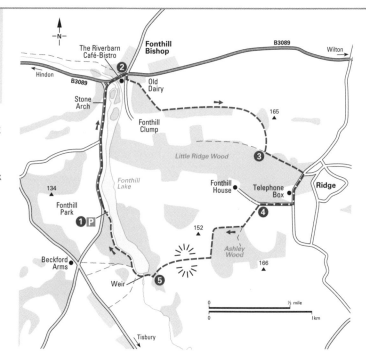

TOLLARD ROYAL Around Rushmore Park

A walk in the heart of Cranborne Chase.

4.5 miles/7.2km 2hrs 30min **Ascent** 616ft/188m ⚠ **Difficulty** 2
Paths Field and woodland paths, bridle paths and tracks, 3 stiles
Map OS Explorer 118 Shaftesbury & Cranborne Chase **Grid ref** ST 944178
Parking By pond in Tollard Royal

❶ Facing pond, turn **L** along metalled track and take waymarked path **R** across footbridge to stile. Follow narrow path half **L** uphill through scrub and along **L-H** field edge. Keep ahead, pass copse, and bear **L** through gates into adjacent field. Keep to **R-H** edge, following electricity poles downhill to gate and stile.
❷ Bear diagonally **L** and steeply descend to gate and junction of paths in valley bottom. Take track **R**, through gate and continue to fork of tracks. Steeply ascend grassy track ahead and beside woodland for 0.5 mile (800m). Bear **R** through trees to metalled lane.
❸ Turn **R**, then **L** before gates to Rushmore Park. Keep to established track, with cameo views across park, heading gently downhill to crossing of paths by golf course.
❹ Turn **R**, pass in front of cottage, and keep to path alongside fairway to redundant gate posts. Pass beside gate posts and keep ahead, soon passing pond and bearing **L** beside woods on **R**.

❺ Bear **R** through gate into woodland and follow yellow waymarker sharp **R** through trees. At first ill-defined, path soon bears **L** to become clear route (yellow arrows) through Brookes Coppice, to reach T-junction with track.
❻ Turn **L**, cross drive and stile opposite, and bear slightly **L** downhill to gate in field corner. In few paces, take 2nd arrowed path sharp **R**.
❼ Follow track through Tinkley Bottom to gate and pass below Rushmore Farm. On passing through 2nd of 2 gateways, turn immediately **L** and walk uphill to pair of gates. Go through **L-H** gate and follow wire fence on **R** through 2 paddocks to reach small steel gate.
❽ Take path ahead and bear diagonally **R** downhill to gate and B3081. Keep ahead into Tollard Royal back to pond and your car.

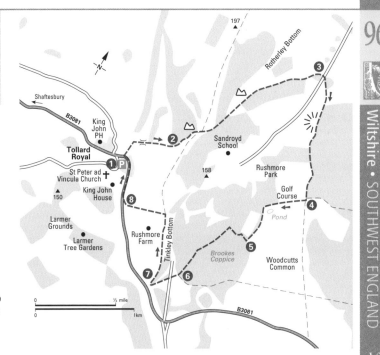

CASTLE COMBE A Picture-Book Village

Through the hilly and wooded By Brook Valley from a famous Wiltshire village.

5.75 miles/9.2km 2hrs 30min **Ascent** 515ft/157m ⚠ **Difficulty** 2

Paths Field and woodland paths and tracks, metalled lanes, 10 stiles
Map OS Explorer 156 Chippenham & Bradford-on-Avon **Grid ref** ST 845776
Parking Free car park just off B4039 at Upper Castle Combe

❶ Leave car park via steps; turn **R**. At T-junction, turn **R** and follow lane into Castle Combe. Keep **L** at Market Cross, then cross By Brook and continue along road to path 'Long Dean', across 2nd bridge on **L**.

❷ Pass through gate and follow path uphill and then beside **R-H** fence above valley (Macmillan Way). Beyond open area, gently ascend through woodland to stile and gate. Cross stile and descend into Long Dean.

❸ Pass mill and, where lane bears **L**, follow track **R** to cross river bridge. At mill house, keep **R** and follow sunken bridleway uphill to gate. Shortly enter sloping pasture and follow defined path around top edge, bearing **L** to reach stile and lane.

❹ Turn **L** and descend to A420 at Ford. Turn **R** along pavement and shortly turn **R** into Park Lane. Climb gravel track and take footpath **L** through squeeze stile.

❺ Keep **R** through pasture and continue through trees to water-meadow in valley bottom. Turn **L**, cross stile and stream and steeply ascend slope ahead of

you, bearing **L** beyond trees towards waymarker post. Follow footpath along top of field to stile and gate, then walk through woodland to gate and the road.

❻ Turn **L**, then immediately **L** again, signposted 'North Wraxall'. Continue for 0.5 mile (800m) and take arrowed bridleway, **R**. Follow track and then, just before gate, keep **R** downhill along sunken path to footbridge to cross Broadmead Brook.

❼ Soon, climb stile on **R** and follow footpath close to river. Cross stile and soon pass beside Nettleton Mill House, bearing **R** to hidden gate. Walk beside stream, cross stile and soon reach golf course.

❽ Turn **R** along track, cross bridge and turn immediately **R**. At gate, follow path **L** below golf fairway. Walk beside wall to stile on **R**. Drop to metalled drive; keep ahead back into Castle Combe. Turn **L** at Market Cross and retrace steps to start.

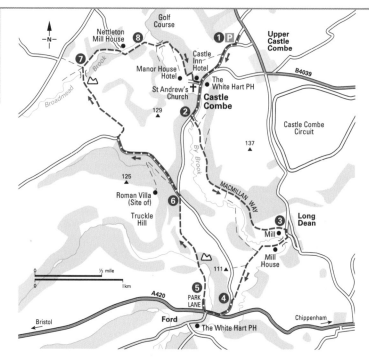

LACOCK Birthplace Of Photography

A stroll around England's finest medieval village with a riverside walk and a visit to Lacock Abbey.

2 miles/3.2km 1hr **Ascent** 16ft/5m ⚠ **Difficulty** 1
Paths Field paths and tracks; some road walking, 4 stiles
Map OS Explorer 156 Chippenham & Bradford-on-Avon **Grid ref** ST 918681
Parking Pay-and-display car park on edge of Lacock; free to National Trust members

❶ From the car park entrance, cross road and follow gravel path into village, passing entrance to Lacock Abbey and Fox Talbot Museum. Turn **R** into East Street opposite Red Lion and walk down to Church Street. Turn **L**, pass At The Sign of the Angel with its magnificent 16th-century doorway and bear **L** into West Street to opposite George Inn. Shortly, follow road **L** into High Street.

❷ Pass National Trust shop and turn **L** to walk back down East Street. Turn **R** along Church Street and turn **L** at Nethercote, in front of St Cyriac's Church, to reach ancient packhorse bridge beside ford across Bide Brook. Follow path beside stream, then up lane beside cottages to reach end of road.

❸ Go through kissing gate on **R** and follow tarmac path across field to gate. Pass stone cottages at Reybridge to lane. Turn **R** along lane, then **R** again to cross bridge over River Avon.

❹ Immediately cross stile on **R** and bear diagonally **L** to far corner where you rejoin riverbank to reach

kissing gate. Walk beside river for 200yds (183m) to stile, and cross field following line of electricity poles to gate. Keep straight on to stile beside gate, and then head towards stone bridge over Avon.

❺ Climb stile and turn **R** across bridge. Join raised pavement and follow it back into village and car park.

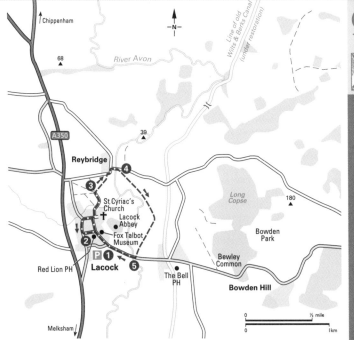

CORSHAM A Wealthy Weaving Town

Explore this unexpected architectural town and adjacent Corsham Park.

4 miles/6.4km 2hrs **Ascent** 114ft/35m ⚠ **Difficulty** 1

Paths Field paths and country lanes, 10 stiles
Map OS Explorer 156 Chippenham & Bradford-on-Avon **Grid ref** ST 871704
Parking Long-stay car park in Newlands Lane

1 Turn **L** out of car park, then **L** again along Post Office Lane to High Street. Turn **L**, pass tourist information centre and turn **R** into Church Street. Pass impressive entrance to Corsham Court, on **L**, and enter St Bartholomew's churchyard.

2 Follow path **L** gate and walk ahead to main path across Corsham Park. Turn **L** and walk along south side of park, passing Corsham Lake, to reach stile and gate. Keep straight on along fenced path beside track to kissing gate and proceed across field to stile and lane.

3 Turn **L**, pass Park Farm, splendid stone farmhouse, on **L** and shortly take waymarked footpath **R** along drive to pass Rose and Unicorn House. Cross stile and follow **R-H** field edge to stile, then bear half **L** to stone stile in field corner. Ignore path arrowed **R** and head straight across field to further stile and lane.

4 Take footpath opposite, bearing half **L** to stone stile to **L** of cottage. Maintain direction, passing to **R**

of spring and go through field entrance to follow path along **L-H** side of field to stile in corner. Turn **L** along road for 0.5 mile (800m) to reach A4.

5 Go through gate in wall on **L** and follow worn path **R**, across centre of parkland pasture to metal kissing gate. Proceed ahead to kissing gate on edge of woodland. Follow wide path to further gate and bear half **R** to stile.

6 Keep ahead on worn path across parkland and along field edge to gate. Continue to further gate with fine views **R** to Corsham Court. Follow path **R** along field edge, then where it curves **R**, bear **L** to join path beside churchyard wall to stile.

7 Turn **L** down avenue of trees to gate and town centre, noting stone almshouses on **L**. Turn **R** along Lacock Road and then **R** again along pedestrianised High Street. Turn **L** back along Post Office Lane to car park.

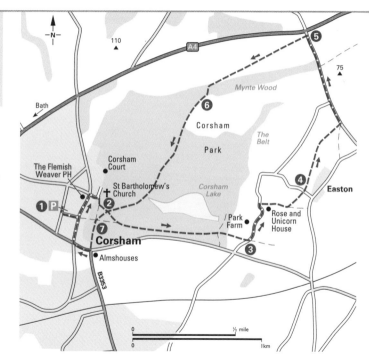

BRADFORD-ON-AVON A Miniature Bath

Combine a visit to this enchanting riverside town with a canal-side walk.

3.25 miles/5.3km 1hr 45min **Ascent** 164ft/50m ⚠ **Difficulty** 1

Paths Towpath, field and woodland paths, metalled lanes
Map OS Explorer156 Chippenham & Bradford-on-Avon **Grid ref** ST 824606
Parking Bradford-on-Avon Station car park (charge)

❶ Walk to end of car park, away from station, and follow path **L** beneath railway and beside River Avon. Enter Barton Farm Country Park and keep to path across grassy area to junction of paths. With packhorse bridge **R**, bear **R**, then **L** to pass to **R** of tithe barn to reach Kennet and Avon Canal.

❷ Turn **R** along towpath, signed to Avoncliff. Cross bridge over canal in 0.5 mile (800m) and follow path **R** to footbridge and gate. Proceed along **R-H** edge to further gate, then bear diagonally **L** uphill away from canal to kissing gate.

❸ Follow path along edge of woodland. Keep to path as it bears **L** uphill through trees to reach lane. Turn **R** and walk steeply downhill to canal at Avoncliff.

❹ Don't cross aqueduct, instead pass Mad Hatter Tea Rooms, descend steps on **R** and pass beneath canal. Keep **R** by The Cross Guns and join towpath towards Bradford-on-Avon. Continue for 0.75 mile (1.2km) to bridge passed on outward route.

❺ Bear off **L** downhill along metalled track and follow it beside River Avon back into Barton Farm Country Park. Cross packhorse bridge and railway and follow walled path uphill and **R** into Barton Orchard. Bear **R** at end down alleyway to Church Street.

❻ Continue ahead past Holy Trinity Church and Church of St Laurence. Cross footbridge and go through St Margaret's car park to road. Turn **R**, then **R** again to station car park.

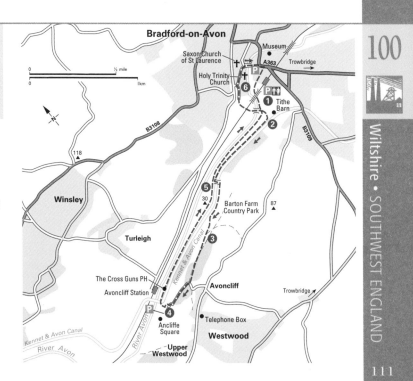

Walking in Safety

All these walks are suitable for any reasonably fit person, but less experienced walkers should try the easier walks first. Route finding is usually straightforward, but you will find that an Ordnance Survey map is a vitasl addition to the route maps and descriptions.

Risks

Although each walk has been researched with a view to minimising the risks to the walkers who follow its route, no walk in the countryside can be considered to be completely free from risk. Walking in the outdoors will always require a degree of common sense and judgement to ensure that it is as safe as possible.

- Be particularly careful on cliff paths and in upland terrain, where the consequences of a slip can be very serious.

- Remember to check tidal conditions before walking along the seashore.

- Some sections of route are by, or cross roads. Take care and remember traffic is a danger even on minor country lanes.

- Be careful around farmyard machinery and livestock, especially if you have children or a dog with you.

- Be aware of the consequences of changes of weather and check the forecast before you set off. Carry spare clothing and a torch if you are walking in the winter months. Remember that the weather can change very quickly at any time of the year, and in moorland and heathland areas, mist and fog can make route finding much harder. Don't set out in these conditions unless you are confident of your navigation skills in poor visibility. In summer remember to take account of the heat and sun; wear a hat and carry spare water.

- On walks away from centres of population you should carry a whistle and survival bag. If you do have an accident requiring the emergency services, make a note of your position as accurately as possible and dial 999.

Mystery Mob
and the
Hidden Treasure

Roger Hurn

Illustrated by
Stik

RISING★STARS

Rising Stars UK Ltd.
7 Hatchers Mews, Bermondsey Street, London SE1 3GS
www.risingstars-uk.com

The right of Roger Hurn to be identified as the author of this work
has been asserted by him in accordance with the Copyright, Design
and Patents Act 1988.

Published 2007
Reprinted 2008, 2012

Text, design and layout © Rising Stars UK Ltd.

Cover design: Button plc
Illustrator: Stik, Bill Greenhead for Illustration
Text design and typesetting: Andy Wilson
Publisher: Gill Budgell
Publishing manager: Sasha Morton
Editor: Catherine Baker
Series consultant: Cliff Moon

British Library Cataloguing in Publication Data.
A CIP record for this book is available from the British Library

ISBN: 978-1-84680-222-5

Printed by Ashford Colour Press Ltd